A Sussex Christmas

This book is dedicated to Bob Copper

A Sussex Christmas

Compiled by Shaun Payne

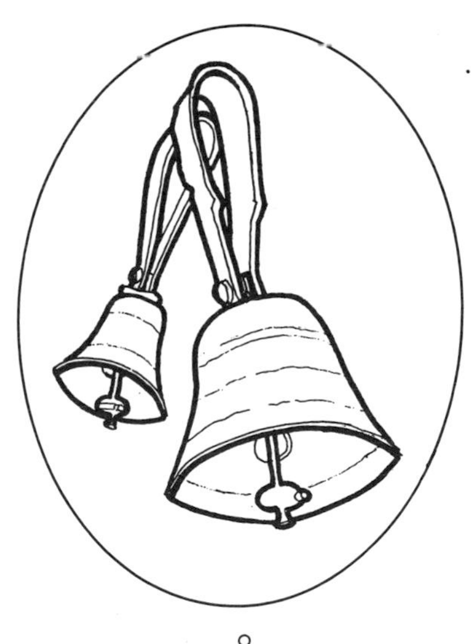

ALAN SUTTON

First published in the United Kingdom in 1990 by
Alan Sutton Publishing Limited · Phoenix Mill · Far Thrupp
Stroud · Gloucestershire

First published in the United States of America in 1991 by
Alan Sutton Publishing Inc · Wolfeboro Falls · NH 03896–0848

British Library Cataloguing in Publication Data

Payne, Shaun
A Sussex Christmas.
1. East Sussex. West Sussex. East & West Sussex.
Christmas, history
I. Title
394.268282094225

ISBN 0-86299-747-X

Library of Congress Cataloging in Publication Data applied for

Cover illustration: Hurrying Home. *(Photograph: Fine Art Photographic Library Limited)*

Typesetting and origination by
Alan Sutton Publishing Limited.
Printed in Great Britain by
Dotesios Printers Limited.

Contents

'Shepherds Arise'

BOB COPPER

In rural Sussex, as in other parts of the south country, the celebration of Christmas has always begun with the singing of carols on Christmas Eve. So, how better, by way of a prologue, to begin this book than with a full-throated Sussex carol, which has been sung time-out-of-mind by an old village family, the Coppers of Rottingdean.

Shepherds arise, be not afraid, with hasty steps prepare
To David's city, sin on earth,
With our blest Infant – with our blest Infant there,
With our blest Infant there, with our blest Infant there.
Sing, sing, all earth, sing, sing, all earth eternal praises sing
To our Redeemer, to our Redeemer and our heavenly King.

Laid in a manger viewed a Child, humility Divine,
Sweet innocent sounds meek and mild.
Grace in his features – grace in his features shine,
Grace in his features shine, grace in his features shine.
Sing, sing, all earth, sing, sing, all earth eternal praises sing
To our Redeemer, to our Redeemer and our heavenly King.

For us the Saviour came on earth, for us his life he gave,
To save us from eternal death
And to raise us from – and to raise us from the grave
To raise us from the grave and to raise us from the grave
Sing, sing, all earth, sing, sing, all earth eternal praises sing
To our Redeemer, to our Redeemer and our heavenly King.

The traditional sheep of the South Downs, seen against a snowscape near Singleton

Turn o' the Year

BOB COPPER

Bob Copper is perhaps the greatest living Sussex writer and folk-singer, a man who loves, thinks and is *Sussex. Now seventy-five, he was born in a flint cottage at Rottingdean, the (then tiny) Downland village where the Copper family had lived since Tudor times. His Uncle John was a shepherd; his father and grandfather bailiffs of the largest of the Rottingdean farms. From them, Bob learned all the jobs expected of a farm boy in those days and the traditions of farm, family and village life. Blessed with an astonishing memory, he has recorded his impressions of the old rural culture of Sussex in two books,* A Song for Every Season *and* Early to Rise, *which are of unrivalled authenticity and accuracy. These books reveal what life was like for village people and show the comfort and joy that Christmas gave to farm folk whose long winters were shaped by short days and often bitter weather on those bleak hills above the sea.*

Our barns they are full, our fields they are clear,
Good luck to our master and friends.
We'll make no more to do but we'll plough and we'll sow
And prepare for the very next year.

Two Young Brethren

As we got further into winter especially if it was frosty there was the yards to be cleared of dung. We had five sheep yards and our home nine stables and the cowstalls to clear of dung, and I have seen over 200 cartload in Court Farm Yard outside the cowstalls where Tudor Close lawn and sundial is now. And then there was the dung from Brighton which was always taken straight from Brighton to the field where it was going to be used and unloaded in a lump which we called the 'mixen'. This was taken out with 3 horses and carts – sometimes if a big laine, – 3 fillers, carter to shelve, or unload, and boys to drive to and from till 2.30 p.m. The fillers would take their dinner with them and when the horses had gone home they had to stop and spread 40 load to fill in their day.

Well this dunging made off with a good bit of our time in the winter and it covered a good many acres with beautiful stuff.

Some dung-spreading was done piece-work. One day Jim was in the store-room filing up with the other chaps to Grand-dad's office to collect what was due to him in the way of wages. He had done some overtime but when it came to his turn he was handed his exact weekly wage. He stood for a while looking at it and Grand-dad said, 'Get on there, mairt, what are y' 'anging about for?'

'We done a bit of overtime this wik, Dad, dung-spreading up Man and Mare.'

'You ben't goin' t' charge me f' that, be ye?'

'Well, we've bin thinkin' of it over,' said Jim, 'and we reckon that bein' 'eavy it's worth three shillings an acre.'

'You come an' see me agin after the wik-end,' said the old man.

On Monday morning he called Jim over. 'I've bin up Man an' Mare and 'ad a look at that 'ere dung you wuz supposed to spread,' he said, 'an' I've bin thinkin' of it over, too. If you go an' spread it agin, I'll pay y' 2/9 an acre.'

After telling me this tale Jim observed thoughtfully, 'You 'ad a job to git one over on my ol' Daddy.'

By this time it was beginning to feel a bit like Christmas. The puddings had been boiled in the copper in the corner of the scullery some weeks before and the boys had started hand-bell ringing and practising the 'Mummer's Play' in the evenings down at the Black Horse. During the week before Christmas they used to visit all the big houses in the village in turn with the bells and the Mummers and were welcomed with plenty of Christmas fare in the way of wine, beer and cake. One night, they were on their way up the High Street making for 'Hillside' where Colonel Phillips and his family and friends were awaiting their arrival. They were all fairly talkative, having spent a considerable time around the punch-bowl at the previous call, and by the time they reached Reading Room Corner Father Christmas and Black Jack were having a heated argument. A few yards further on Father Christmas gave Black Jack a swipe round the head with his holly bush and Jack, forgetting for a moment the 'peace and goodwill' part of the Christmas message, retaliated with his birch broom. They 'leathered into each other like a couple of tom-cats' but after a short while were separated and prevailed upon to proceed in an orderly fashion. On being admitted to Colonel Phillip's parlour, however, Father Christmas, who had still not quite regained his composure, stepped through the door and blurted out with an air of defiance, 'In come I ol' Father Chris'mus, be I walcum or be I bain't?' Then in the lighted interior of the room they could see that his cottonwool beard was all askew and hanging from one ear, and his holly bush, which was his badge of office, had been broken and stripped of all but one or two leaves. Black Jack, too, showed signs of battle. He had had a slight nose-bleed and there were only two or three twigs of birch left on his broom. The company of players, however, made a brave recovery and the audience accepted these little

Gathering mistletoe for Christmas 1937 at Camelsdale. The mistletoe had been covered over with an old lace curtain to prevent the birds getting at it

discrepancies in the spirit of the occasion. After the beer jugs and wine decanter had gone the rounds the play ran its course and with wishes all round for a merry holiday they all parted on the best of terms.

It was under the tiny roof of Grand-dad's cottage at Northgate that the whole family met at Christmas time, the one and sometimes only occasion in the year when they all got together at the same time, in spite of the fact that most of them lived in the village. There was, however, one exception. Jim had an uncle that lived just off the High Street who was not of a very sociable disposition. He was happier spending his evenings sitting on the settle in the corner of the Black Horse tap-room in the company of his beer pot and clay pipe. He was, it seems, a 'queer ol' cove' who habitually wore a smock, 'Lord above knows what he wore underneath', comments Jim, 'rags I shouldn't wonder.' He was also an inveterate tobacco-chewer, as were many of his contemporaries. 'He didn't like comin' to our place,' said Jim, "cos he wouldn't be allowed to spit in the fire. Anyway,' he added scornfully, "e couldn't sing.'

Grand-dad, being foreman on the farm and a man of some substance in the village, kept a good table all through the year but at Christmas time it creaked beneath the weight of extra drink and foodstuffs. There was always a huge turkey of about twenty-five lbs or more so that you 'could cut an' come agin' and the farmer every year gave him a sixteen-lb round of local beef as a seasonable gift. These two items alone were far too large for the cottage oven and so the boys had to take them down to Allwork's the bakers, who always lit the ovens specially for the Christmas morning roastings. By about midday that small cottage was fairly bulging with people. There were aunts and uncles, cousins and second-cousins, aunts' brothers and uncles' sisters and all the motley gang of various ages that were connected, by whatever tenuous relationships, to the family home. Long trails of star-leafed ivy festooned the dresser and sprigs of holly sprouted from behind the pictures on the wall. To mark the occasion Grand-dad would be wearing his fancy waistcoat, the one with the knitted panels in red and green, bisected vertically by a curving line of small round buttons like cat's eyes, and horizontally by a gold 'Albert' watch-chain which looped away in opposite directions from one of the central buttons to disappear into two pockets on either side of his sturdy frontage. There would be a lively exchange of family and village trivialities going on while glasses of sherry or 'hot toddy' were sipped in a log-blazing cigar-filled atmosphere.

About one o'clock, the lads went down to the bakehouse to

see if the bird was fit for the table. Being such a giant of a bird the turkey was very often the last one out of the oven and, as the bakehouse was so conveniently close to the Black Horse – the back door of which was almost within arm's reach – they would wait in the tap-room until the baker gave them a shout. By the time this happened they had probably consumed two or three glasses of Uncle Tommy's strong Christmas Ale. That was a powerful good beer, and as Jim said, 'Carrying the beef and turkey home after a couple of glasses of that was a bit of a dido. You 'ad to take middlin' short steps sometimes to keep from spillin' the drippin'.'

Grand-dad was fortunate in that he had learnt how to turn water – and pond water at that – if not into wine, at least into beer. In return for allowing the various breweries on their weekly visits to the village to fill up their steam-driven drays with water at the farm ponds he was rewarded in kind. From one he had a regular supply throughout the year of mild beer in casks, which were stolleged up in the cupboard under the stairs, and at Christmas time this was supplemented with a cask of XXXX Ale, and a further cask of double stout for the ladies. From another brewer he received a cask of specially brewed Christmas ale. 'Dan'l that would make your ol' eyes strike fire,' said Jim, 'That was like rhubub wine – lovely.'

Grand-dad, with his deep booming delivery, said grace much slower than usual which, together with the sight of the laden table, added weight and significance to his words,

'For what we are about to receive may the Lord make us *truly* thankful.'

There was always something rather odd about tea-time on Christmas Day. It seemed more of a ceremony than a meal. Whereas no one could imagine Christmas Day without its lavish display of a huge iced cake, sweet and savoury sandwiches, chocolate biscuits and cream confections and

homemade mince pies, neither could they raise the slightest enthusiasm for it. They just were not hungry.

While teacups were drained in quick succession, the mountains of foodstuffs remained practically untouched. The Christmas cake was pecked and nibbled at as a sort of ritual but the mince pies remained a problem. Each mince pie eaten, it used to be said, ensured one happy month in the ensuing year and although from January until about April or May could be accounted for fairly comfortably, the fate of high summer would be in the balance until finally after August or September, despite the loosening of belts and the unfastening of top trouser buttons, the struggle would have to be abandoned and the remainder of the year reluctantly left to chance.

After tea and after the beer jugs had been passed round to 'wet their whistles', Grand-dad seated in his armchair on one side of the fire would nod gravely to Uncle Tom on the other and with no more ado would launch into the first carol. All the company of uncles and aunts, brothers, sisters and cousins would join in with their home-spun harmonies and variations until the little cottage fairly shook with sound. Christmas hymns followed carols one after another and the natural unsophisticated voices raised in simple worship expressed the pleasure and gratitude of everyone for being all together on yet another Christmas night.

'Shepherds arise, be not afraid, with hasty steps prepare
To David's city, sin on earth,
With our blest Infant – with our blest Infant there,
With our blest Infant there, with our blest Infant there.
Sing, sing, all earth, sing, sing, all earth eternal praises sing
To our Redeemer, to our Redeemer and our Heavenly King.'

Shepherds Arise

Thus the earlier part of the evening was spent in singing sacred music and as Jim said, 'If you was fed up with beer by nine o'clock you'd have to sit and wait for anything stronger. For my old Daddy wouldn't allow any wines or spirits on the table until half-past nine.' By that time the repertoire of Christmas music was about exhausted and the 'old songs' would follow, while passers-by paused and stood for a while outside to listen. Brasser and his family were keeping up Christmas in the traditional way once again.

At eleven o'clock they would shut down for supper. The first thing to be put on the table was a 12 lb ham which was an annual present from the farmer's wife to Granny. Then the round of beef and, what was probably the favourite of all, a great, cold, boned-rabbit pie all set in thick jelly with flank of bacon and hard-boiled eggs. If Granny had not got a pie dish large enough she would bake two. Grand-dad would carve the ham and beef and when everybody had got a plateful, he would sit down to his own and then start singing.

'O, don't you remember a long time ago
Those two little babies their names I don't know,
They strayed away one fine summer's day,
Those two little babies got lost on their way.
Pretty babes in the wood, pretty babes in the wood,
O, don't you remember those babes in the wood.'

Babes in the Wood

This song was always sung during supper on Christmas night and by an ingenious method of alternating the singing and eating, the continuity of both the song and the supper was maintained. The song would swing from one side of the table to the other like a shuttlecock. Roughly one half of the singers, with food-laden forks poised in front of them, taking

An example of unredeemed Edwardian sentiment. Embossed holly, flecked with snow, frames the girls and Santa

the first two lines of a verse while the other half hastily devoured a mouthful of rabbit pie in time to take the last two, on the completion of which all had to be clear for the whole company to join in the chorus. One cannot help thinking that in the interests of everyone's digestion it was a good thing the song had only three verses.

On Boxing Day in the morning the Brookside Harriers always met on the Green opposite Down House where Mr Steyning Beard, the Master, lived. At 11 a.m. sharp Grandad would pour himself a strong hot gin, light a cigar in his meerschaum and amber holder and 'doddle off down to the meet'. After the stirrup cup had gone round to the gentlemen and the jugs of beer had been handed out the hunt would move off to draw their first cover. They could always rely on one of the shepherds, who were well acquainted with the wild life on the downs, to tell them where they would be likely to find a hare and they would pay him four shillings for his information.

The hunt usually returned at about 4 p.m. and after they had had time to have dinner, Grand-dad, Uncle Tommy, John and Jim would go to Down House and stand on the lawn and start singing carols. Jim said, 'We usually started off on something pretty easy as we had all had a bit of a stinger the night before and usually felt a little bit ornery.' By the time they had got to about the third verse, Mr Steyning Beard would open the door and say, 'Come inside, Jim, come in Tommy – all of you, and let's have some decent hunting songs. We can hear those other things when we go to church on Sunday mornings.' When they got inside there would be a big log-fire flaring away on the hearth with the gentlemen all sitting round still in their hunting gear and on the table would be a 'damn gurt bowl of punch', piping hot. The master would ladle some out and say, 'Come on, you must have some punch before you start. You can't sing on an empty stomach y'know.'

And so they would sing all the old hunting songs and many others well on into the evening.

'You gentlemen of high renown come listen to me
Who take delight in fox and hounds of every high degree.
A story true to you I'll tell concerning of a fox,
In Oxford town in Oxfordshire there lived some mighty hounds.'

Gentlemen of High Renown

The wheel of the year had run round another full circle – from lambing-time to the long, hot sheep-shearing days of June along through haying and harvest and on to the dark, dung-spreading days of December. Each season bringing its own particular tasks and long, hard days of labour. O, yes, there was plenty of work and worry but there was also a song for every season and always a stout heart and a lusty voice to sing it.

The Sailor's Carol

HILAIRE BELLOC

The Four Men *is an extraordinary tale, best summed up by its subtitle, 'A Farrago' – that is, a 'hotch-potch'. It is a story of a walk across Sussex made in 1902 by the four men of the title: Grizzlebeard, the Sailor, the Poet and the*

narrator, 'Myself'. Setting off from the George at Robertsbridge on the thirtieth of October, 'Myself' and Grizzlebeard are soon joined in their westward tramp by the others, whom they meet by chance, until they finally part company at Harting, near the Hampshire border, on the second of November: a journey of four days. Not, you may think, very promising stuff for a Christmas book. But a man may sing of Christmas at any season, especially if he is a sailor intent on teasing a poet for making verse – and bad *verse, at that! – about spring when it is autumn. At this point, towards the end of the third day, they have almost reached Duncton.*

The Poet 'It seems to me you are not of the trade; you are choppy in verse, very short-winded, halting; spavined, I think.'
The Sailor 'Why! I have sung the longest songs of you all! And since you challenge me, I will howl you one quite rotund and complete, but I warn you, your hair will stand on end!'
Grizzlebeard 'I dread the Sailor. He is blasphemous and lewd.'
The Sailor 'Judge when you have heard. It is a carol.'
The Poet 'But it is not Christmas.'
The Sailor 'Neither is it spring, yet by licence we sang our songs of springtime – and for that. . . Well, let me *seize* you all. It has a title – not my own. We call this song 'Noël'.'
Myself (*prettily*) 'And I congratulate you, Sailor, on your whimsical originality and pretty invention in titles.'
The Sailor –

'Noël! Noël! Noël! Noël!
A Catholic tale have I to tell:
And a Christian song have I to sing
While all the bells in Arundel ring.

'I pray good beef and I pray good beer
This holy night of all the year,
But I pray detestable drink for them
That give no honour to Bethlehem.

'May all good fellows that here agree
Drink Audit Ale in heaven with me,
And may all my enemies go to hell!
Noël! Noël! Noël! Noël!
May all my enemies go to hell!
Noël! Noël!'

Grizzlebeard 'Rank blasphemy as I said, and heresy, which is worse. For at Christmas we should in particular forgive our enemies.'
The Sailor 'I do. This song is about those that do not forgive me.'

This portrait was enclosed in a Christmas card, *c.* 1880. Sending family photographs was common practice in the late nineteenth century

The Poet 'And it is bad verse, like all the rest.'
The Sailor 'Go drown yourself in milk and water; it is great, hefty howl-verse, as strong and meaty as that other of mine was lovely and be-winged.'
Grizzlebeard 'What neither the Poet nor you seem to know, Sailor, is that the quarrels of versifiers are tedious to standers-by, so let us go into the Cricketers' Arms and eat as you say, in God's name, and occupy ourselves with something pleasanter than the disputed lyric.'
Myself 'Very well then, let us go into the Cricketers' Arms. . . .'

Stir-up Sunday and Gooding Day

JACQUELINE SIMPSON

For children half the joy of Christmas lies in the anticipation, and in most Sussex families the first excitement is stirring the ingredients for the Christmas pudding! Here Jacqueline Simpson, who has done so much to record our County's folk ways, tells the story behind 'Stir-up Sunday' and of the needs that once made Gooding Day important to the Sussex poor.

The last Sunday before Advent has long been known, and still is, as 'Stir-up Sunday'. The collect for the day begins 'Stir up, O Lord, we beseech Thee, the hearts of Thy faithful people . . .' and this was jokingly associated with the idea that it was time for the housewives to prepare the mixtures for the Christmas puddings and pies, if they were to have time to grow rich and mellow by waiting. So, on the way home, the children sang:

> Stir up, we beseech thee,
> The pudding in the pot,
> And when we get home,
> We'll eat it all hot.

Next day, the grocers' windows would be filled with raisins, currants, spices, almonds, dried fruit, and all the other ingredients needed, and the women would set about their task. The actual stirring of these mixtures was a pleasant family ritual in which everyone took part. When they were already partially blended, everyone would be called in to help stir – mother first, then father, then the children in order of age, then all other members of the household, including servants, if any. Even babies stirred; the author has been informed that she stirred her first Christmas pudding in 1931, at the age of one. The way it was done was important; one must use a wooden spoon and turn it sunwise, from left to right – some say, because Christ's manger was of wood and because the Magi travelled sunwise as they searched for Bethlehem. And one should stir silently, with one's eyes shut, and make a secret wish.

The mince-pie mixture was also made in the week after Stir-up Sunday, and it too had some legends attached to it. For instance, many women put a little powdered rosemary into the mincemeat (which at one time included real meat, as well as

One of George Garland's most popular photographs: a little girl enjoys a wish as she stirs the Christmas pudding, while the cat, ever hopeful, looks on. A scene, doubtless, from 'Stir-up Sunday'

fruit and spices) because of the tale that when Mary fled into Egypt with her Child, a rosemary bush by the wayside held out its branches for her to hang out the baby's clothes to dry on. At one time, too, the pies were baked in special little oblong tins with rounded corners, representing a cradle – no true Sussex cook would have made a round mince pie! The spicy filling represented the gifts of the Magi.

December was, naturally, dominated by the approach of Christmas, but just before the great day there is another feast that was once of importance to the poorer sections of the community – St Thomas' Day, 21 December, popularly known as Gooding Day, or, sometimes, Doling Day or Mumping Day ('mumping' being an old slang word for 'begging'). As M.A. Lower says, writing in 1861:

Formerly, the old women of every parish went from house to house to beg something wherewith to provide for the festivities of Christmas. The miller gave each dame a little flour, the grocer a few raisins, the butcher an odd bit of beef, and so on. From persons not in trade a donation in money was expected.

Lower asserted that the custom was in his time 'almost obsolescent', but in this he was certainly mistaken; several other writers mention it as prevalent in their own districts later in the nineteenth century, and indeed it was not wholly extinct even in living memory – the hardships of the elderly poor, especially widows, are not so easily disposed of. Moreover, 'going a-gooding' was and remained a serious custom, springing from real need, unlike the more light-hearted 'clemmening', Guy Fawkes begging, or carol singing nowadays, though the latter, interestingly, is now often done to raise money for charities.

The type of goods distributed varied. At Horsham, in the nineteenth century, the gentry used to give out food, warm clothing, and sometimes money; at Lewes in the 1870s, surplus stocks of discarded clothes and hats would be left outside certain shops, and anyone who needed them could take them; at Mayfield, where the custom still existed in 1903, there was one old gentleman who had made it his life-long habit to save up all the fourpenny pieces which came his way throughout the year, to distribute them to the old women on Gooding Day. In one village, the name of which is unfortunately not given in the source, the widows went to church on this day with sprigs of holly or mistletoe, which they handed to anyone who gave them money – a pleasant fiction, no doubt, to soften stark 'charity' into a form of 'selling'. Similarly at Beeding, in the first half of the nineteenth century, the vicar used to sit at his study window handing out half-crowns to any old woman who 'sold' him a sprig of evergreens. At Arundel, on the other hand, the distribution of alms was official; the money given out was the yearly interest on the sum of £15 which had been found on the body of a dead tramp in 1824, and which had been put into trust for this purpose.

Sussex Woods in Winter

RICHARD JEFFERIES

A walk through the beech hangers and Wealden forests is a fascinating experience at any season, but on those winter days when wind-swept marshes are too bleak and the Downland 'breeze' too bracing the Sussex woods offer the walker some shelter and much to see. Richard Jefferies, the Victorian naturalist, fell under their spell while he was living in Brighton.

The lost leaves measure our years; they are gone as the days are gone, and the bare branches silently speak of a new year, slowly advancing to its buds, its foliage, and fruit. Deciduous trees associate with human life as this yew never can. Clothed in its yellowish-green needles, its tarnished green, it knows

no hope or sorrow; it is indifferent to winter, and does not look forward to summer. With their annual loss of leaves, and renewal, oak and elm and ash and beech seem to stand by us and to share our thoughts. There is no wind at the edge of the wood, and the few flakes of snow that fall from the overcast sky flutter as they drop, now one side higher and then the other, as the leaves did in the still hours of autumn. The delicacy of the outer boughs of the great trees visible against the dark background of cloud is as beautiful in its own way as the massed foliage of summer. Each slender bough is drawn out to a line; line follows line as shade grows under the pencil, but each of these lines is separate. Great boles of beech, heavy timber at the foot thus end at their summits in the lightest and most elegant pencilling. Where the birches are tall, sometimes the number and closeness of these bare sprays causes a thickening almost as if there were leaves there. The leaves, in fact, when they come, conceal the finish of the trees; they give colour, but they hide the beautiful structure under them. Each tree at a distance is recognizable by its particular lines; the ash, for instance, grows with its own marked curve.

Some flakes of snow have remained on this bough of spruce, pure white on dull green. Sparingly dispersed, the snow can be seen falling far ahead between the trunks; indeed, the white dots appear to increase the distance the eye can penetrate; it sees farther because there is something to catch the glance. Nothing seems left for food in the woods for bird or animal. Some ivy berries and black privet berries remain, a few haws may be found; for the rest, it is gone; the squirrels have had the nuts, the acorns were taken by the jays, rooks, and pheasants. Bushels of acorns, too, were collected by hand as food for the fallow deer in the park. A great fieldfare rises, like a lesser pigeon; fieldfares often haunt the verge of woods, while the redwing thrushes go out into the meadows.

Fallow deer in Petworth Park at Christmas time

Some little green stays on the mounds where the rabbits creep and nibble the grasses. Cinquefoil remains green though faded, and wild parsley the freshest looking of all; plantain leaves are found under shelter of brambles, and the dumb nettles, though the old stalks are dead, have living leaves at the ground. Grey-veined ivy trails along, here and there is a frond of hart's-tongue fern, though withered at the tip, and greenish grey lichen grows on the exposed stumps of trees. These together give a green tint to the mound, which is not so utterly devoid of colour as the season of the year might indicate. Where they fail, brown brake fern fills the spaces between the brambles; and in a moist spot the bunches of rushes are composed half of dry stalks, and half of green. Stems of willow-herb, four feet high, still stand, and tiny long-tailed tits perch sideways on them. Above, on the bank, another species of willow-herb has died down to a short stalk, from which springs a living branch, and at its end is one pink flower. A dandelion is opening on the same sheltered bank; farther on the gorse is sprinkled with golden spots of bloom. A flock of greenfinches starts from the bushes, and their colour shows against the ruddy wands of the osier-bed over which they fly. The path winds round the edge of the wood, where a waggon track goes up the hill; it is deeply grooved at the foot of the hill. These tracks wear deeply into the chalk just where the ascent begins. The chalk adheres to the shoes like mortar, and for some time after one has left it each footstep leaves a white mark on the turf. On the ridge the low trees and bushes have an outline like the flame of a candle in a draught – the wind has blown them till they have grown fixed in that shape. In an oak across the ploughed field a flock of wood-pigeons have settled; on the furrows there are chaffinches, and larks rise and float a few yards farther away. The snow has ceased, and though there is no wind on the surface, the clouds high above have opened somewhat, not sufficient for the sun to shine, but to prolong the already closing afternoon a few minutes. If the sun shines to-morrow morning the lark will soar and sing, though it is January, and the quick note of the chaffinch will be heard as he perches on the little branches projecting from the trunks of trees below the great boughs. Thrushes sing every mild day in December and January, entirely irrespective of the season, also before rain.

Christmas Hardships

ROBERT TRESSELL

Robert Tressell, a house painter who lived in Hastings before the First World War, might have written 'Christmas Day in the Workhouse' had he been a poet. Instead, in his novel, The Ragged Trousered Philanthropists, *he gives us glimpses of the hardships endured by the Hastings poor during 'what is usually called the festive season – possibly because at this period of the year a greater number of people are suffering from hunger and cold than at any other time.'*

For the rest of the week, Owen continued to work down at the yard with Sawkins, Crass, and Slyme, painting some of the ladders, steps and other plant belonging to the firm. These things had to have two coats of paint and the name Rushton & Co. written on them. As soon as they had got some of them second-coated, Owen went on with the writing, leaving the painting for the others, so as to share the work as fairly as possible. Several times during the week one or other of them was taken away to do some other work; once Crass and Slyme had to go and wash off and whiten a ceiling somewhere, and several times Sawkins was sent out to assist the plumbers.

Every day some of the men who had been 'stood off' called at

the yard to ask if any other 'jobs' had 'come in'. From these callers they heard all the news. Old Jack Linden had not succeeded in getting anything to do at the trade since he was trying to earn a little money by hawking bloater from house to house. As for Philpot, *he* said that he had been round to nearly all the firms in the town and none of them had any work to speak of.

Newman – the man whom the reader will remember was sacked for taking too much pains with his work – had been arrested and sentenced for a month's imprisonment because he had not been able to pay his poor rates, and the Board of Guardians were allowing his wife three shillings a week to maintain herself and the three children. Philpot had been to see them, and she told him that the landlord was threatening to turn them into the street; he would have seized their furniture and sold it if it had been worth the expense of the doing.

'I feel ashamed of meself,' Philpot added in confidence to Owen, 'when I think of all the money I chuck away on beer. If it wasn't for that, I shouldn't be in such a hole meself now, and I might be able to lend 'em a 'elpin' 'and.'

'It ain't so much that I likes the beer, you know,' he continued; it's the company. When you ain't got no 'ome, in a manner o' speakin', like me, the pub's about the only place where you can get a little enjoyment. But you ain't very welcome there unless you spends your money.'

'Is the three shillings all they have to live on?'

'I think she goes out charin' when she can get it,' replied Philpot, 'but I don't see as she can do a great deal o' that with three young 'uns to look after, and from what I hear of it she's only just got over a illness and ain't fit to do much.'

'My God!' said Owen.

'I'll tell you what,' said Philpot. 'I've been thinking we might get up a bit of a subscription for 'em. There's several

chaps in work what knows Newman, and if they was each to give a trifle we could get enough to pay for a Christmas dinner, anyway. I've brought a sheet of foolscap with me, and I was goin' to ask you to write out the heading for me.'

As there was no pen available at the workshop, Philpot waited till four o'clock and then accompanied Owen home, where the heading of the list was written. Owen put his name down for a shilling and Philpot his for a similar amount.

Philpot stayed to tea and accepted an invitation to spend Christmas Day with them, and to come to Frankie's party on the Monday after.

The next morning Philpot brought the list to the yard and Crass and Slyme put their names down for a shilling each, and Sawkins for threepence it being arranged that the money was to be paid on pay-day – Christmas Eve. In the meantime, Philpot was to see as many as he could of those who were in work at other firms and get as many subscriptions as possible.

At pay-time on Christmas Eve Philpot turned up with the list and Owen and the others paid him the amounts they had put their names down for. From other men he had succeeded in obtaining nine and sixpence, mostly in sixpences and threepences. Some of this money he had already received, but for the most part he had made appointments with the subscribers to call at their homes that evening. It was decided that Owen should accompany him and also go with him to hand over the money to Mrs Newman.

It took them nearly three hours to get in all the money, for the places they had to go to were in different localities, and in one or two cases they had to wait because their man had not yet come home, and sometimes it was not possible to get away without wasting a little time in talk. In three instances those who had put their names for threepence increased the amounts to sixpence and one who had promised sixpence gave a shilling. There were two items of threepence each which they

did not get at all, the individuals who had put their names down having gone upon the drunk. Another cause of delay was that they met or called on several other men who had not yet been asked for a subscription, and there were several others – including some members of the Painters' Society whom Owen had spoken to during the week – who had promised him to give a subscription. In the end they succeeded in increasing the total amount to nineteen and ninepence, and they then put threehalfpence each to make it up to a pound.

The Newmans lived in a small house the rent of which was six shillings per week and taxes. To reach the house one had to go down a dark and narrow passage between two shops, the

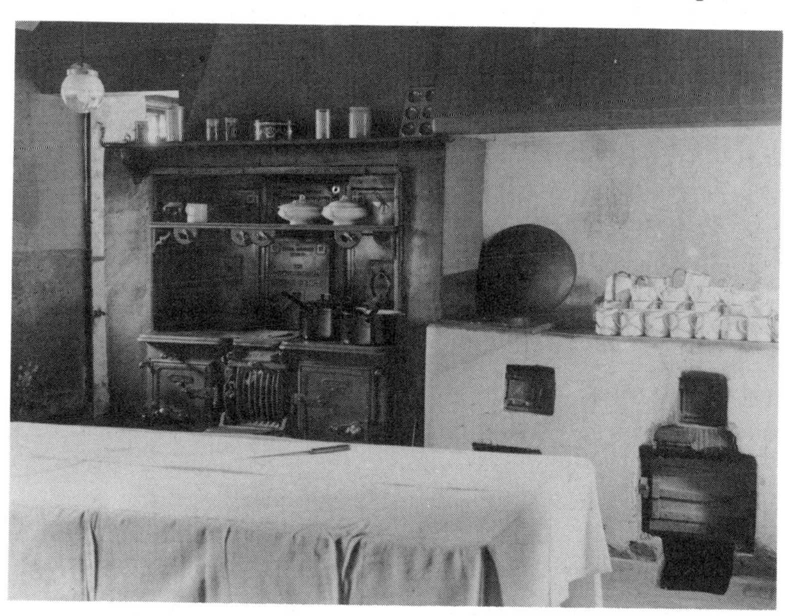

Fear of the 'work-hus' haunted rural and urban poor alike in Sussex until long after the First World War. This photograph shows a re-furbished workhouse kitchen in 1930, but gives no hint of the humiliation and terror suffered by those hapless enough to end their days there

house being in a kind of well, surrounded by the high walls of the back parts of larger buildings – chiefly business premises and offices. The air did not circulate very freely in this place, and the rays of the sun never reached it. In the summer the atmosphere was close and foul with the various odours which came from the back-yards of the adjoining buildings, and in the winter it was dark and damp and gloomy, a culture-ground for bacteria and microbes. The majority of those who profess to be desirous of preventing and curing the disease called consumption must be either hypocrites or fools, for they ridicule the suggestion that it is necessary first to cure and prevent the poverty that compels badly clothed and half-starved human beings to sleep in such dens as this.

The front door opened into the living-room or, rather, kitchen, which was dimly lighted by a small paraffin lamp on the table, where were also some tea-cups and saucers, each of a different pattern, and the remains of a loaf of bread. The wallpaper was old and discoloured; a few almanacs and unframed prints were fixed to the walls, and on the mantelshelf were some cracked and worthless vases and ornaments. At one time they had possessed a clock and an overmantel and some framed pictures, but they had all been sold to obtain money to buy food. Nearly everything of any value had been parted with for the same reason – the furniture, the pictures, the bedclothes, the carpet and the oilcloth, piece by piece, nearly everything that had once constituted the home – had been either pawned or sold to buy food or to pay rent during the times when Newman was out of work – periods that had recurred during the last few years with constantly increasing frequency and duration. Now there was nothing left but these few old broken chairs and the deal table which no one would buy; and upstairs, the wretched bedsteads and mattresses whereon they slept at night, covering themselves with worn-out remnants of blankets and the clothes they wore during the day.

In answer to Philpot's knock, the door was opened by a little girl about seven years old, who at once recognised Philpot, and called out his name to her mother, and the latter came also to the door, closely followed by two other children, a little, fragile-looking girl about three, and a boy about five years of age, who held on to her skirt and peered curiously at the visitors. Mrs Newman was about thirty, and her appearance confirmed the statement of Philpot that she had only just recovered from an illness; she was very white and thin and dejected-looking. When Philpot explained the object of their visit and handed her the money, the poor woman burst into tears, and the two smaller children – thinking that this piece of paper betokened some fresh calamity – began to cry also. They remembered that all their troubles had been preceded by the visits of men who brought pieces of paper, and it was rather difficult to reassure them.

Courtesy

HILAIRE BELLOC

No anthology of Sussex literature would be complete without some of Belloc's poetry – not, this time, an ale-house song, nor even verse in praise of Sussex, but Belloc in religious mood: profound, reflective, quietly celebrating the joy and sorrow of Christ's coming.

A Christmas Day portrait, taken by George Garland in 1932, of Mr and Mrs Stephen Clarke, of Coultershaw, near Petworth, who were celebrating their diamond wedding. They had lived 53 years of their married life in the same house

Of Courtesy, it is much less
Than Courage of Heart or Holiness,
Yet in my Walks it seems to me
That the Grace of God is in Courtesy.

On Monks I did in Storrington fall,
They took me straight into their Hall;
I saw Three Pictures on a wall,
And Courtesy was in them all.

The first the Annunciation;
The second the Visitation;
The third the Consolation,
Of God that was Our Lady's Son.

The first was of Saint Gabriel;
On Wings a-flame from Heaven he fell;
And as he went upon one knee
He shone with Heavenly Courtesy.

Our Lady out of Nazareth rode
It was Her month of heavy load;
Yet was her face both great and kind,
For Courtesy was in Her Mind.

The third it was our Little Lord,
Whom all the Kings in arms adored;
He was so small you could not see
His large intent of Courtesy.

Our Lord, that was Our Lady's Son,
Go bless you, People, one by one;
My Rhyme is written, my work is done.

Christmas Peace

MAUDE ROBINSON

Maude Robinson's memoir, A Southdown Farm in the Sixties, *is one of the joys of my Sussex bookshelf. Maude, born in 1859, grew up on her father's sheep farm at Saddlescombe, a hamlet in the lee of the Downs near Pyecombe. Hers was a secure, happy and unhurried childhood, rich in the innocent adventures of country life which she shared with her brothers and sisters and in the freedom with which they roamed the Downs.*

The Robinsons were Quakers so it is not surprising that Maude's book is pervaded with an unspoken peace that flows from the inner life of prayer. There is a hint, too, of that deep quiet of old Sussex before the ugly noise of motor traffic ruptured the life-giving silence of even the remotest lanes and byways, a tranquility which made possible a richness of being and belonging scarcely imaginable today.

What would modern young people think of the utterly quiet life on the Downs in winter, shut in by snow or rain, with no neighbours to associate with, no wireless, no gramophone, no piano (for we were a Quaker household) until later one appeared in the school-room simultaneously with a German governess? Yet we were perfectly content and happy and never thought of our life as dull. Our parents never craved for more amusement, and the quiet life was the usual thing for farmers in those days.

The long winter evenings were always made cheerful and happy by our parents. The substantial tea – the last meal – was at six o'clock, and almost all the food was home grown. A grist of wheat was sent to Ballard's white windmill at Patcham and brought back as flour. From this the large loaves were kneaded, and baked in a perfect cavern of an oven in the old Tudor end of the house, the large plain cakes in the same way, and we had plenty of jam from the fruitful garden. The butter also was home-made, but not the cheese which always figured at tea time, sometimes Dutch cheese like a magenta football, for which we children had a special appreciation. The table cleared, two good oil lamps were placed upon it, and we all sat round at our different employments, father with his book and paper and with his tired feet to the blazing wood fire, and mother with her overflowing workbasket, for eight active country children made abundance of sewing. She used to threaten to make me a leather frock! But at Christmas 1863 a London uncle presented her with that wonderful new invention, a sewing machine. It was a large clumsy square thing in a walnut wood case – a 'Wheeler and Wilson' lock-stitch. It had a curved needle, most difficult to adjust, and was subject to irregular moods and tensions, yet it was an enormous help, for in those days every curtain, sheet and pillow case was made at home, as well as shirts and frocks. Few houses had a sewing machine then.

Father would sometimes turn from the fire to give the boys help with their chess – a very favourite game which resulted in all four becoming excellent players in after life. We had draughts and dominoes and a home-made card game called 'Families' in which we demanded of each other 'Bun the Baker's wife', and 'Bone the Butcher's son', and thought it very amusing. Ordinary playing cards were never seen. We did not know such things existed! But my chief recollection of a winter evening's toy was waste paper! We cut out figures and

An unusual Victorian Christmas card made in the form of a fan. The six separate leaves of card with gold embossed lettering and fine colours could be opened or closed as with a real fan

houses with doors and windows to open; we folded it into boats, and cocked hats, and elaborate though useless boxes. Waste envelopes were turned to draw pictures on the back, and as we grew older mother would show us how to make acrostics and simple rhyming games. Can it be believed there were no illustrated advertisements in the sixties? The shipping news was headed by a tiny ship, not larger than a postage stamp, and these we cut out as 'pictures'. Then 'Glenfield Starch' began to insert in magazines two advertisements, with pictures of Queen Victoria and Princess Alexandra. These were seized with joy, and daubed with all the colours of the rainbow from our little cedar boxes of stony cakes of paint.

There was always one break in the evening. We heard the door open and a step in the hall and one of the little ones would be told to 'Call Pelling in and set a chair for him'. Then

the old foreman, whom father called 'One of Nature's gentlemen', would come in and take his seat modestly by the door to receive orders as to what each man on the farm was to do next day. He was a nice-looking old man, with thick grey curls and always a tidy linen round frock, embroidered on breast and shoulders by the skilful hands of his daughter. He was 'no scholard', although he had learned to read from his children, but he had the marvellous memory of those days and although master and man discussed a number of plans of work each man was in the right place next morning. Sometimes he would bring news from the outer world from which the heavy wooden shutters had closed us in. 'The foxes was just about barkin' up in the furze', he would say, and we rushed out to hear them. Once I remember his news was of 'northern lights', and from the carriage drive we saw the sky one glorious crimson glow of the Aurora Borealis.

Our evening amusements were always quiet ones, . . .

* * *

Our party on winter evenings was having all the children of the workmen to tea. They arrived shy and solemn, their faces shining with much application of yellow soap, and their hair sleekly greased – probably with lard. We could not blame them, for in the sixties we all used 'pomatum', but ours came from the hairdressers, scented, and in coloured glass pots. Tea in the kitchen wore off some of the shyness of our guests and then came games in the school room, such as 'Hunt the slipper' when a little impromptu conversation between cobbler and customer was received as exquisite wit. To finish there was a Christmas tree and what a simple and inexpensive joy it was! A home-made garment for each, pinafore, hood, or scarf, a bag of marbles, a penny Dutch doll gaily dressed, with a few bags of sweets, and coloured candles.

A small Victorian card with embossed border and 'frame' surrounding the picture of the two singing robins

One year we sought to make a variation by putting the gifts in the sack of a very mild version of Father Christmas, but it was not a success. The unsophisticated little natives who had never seen or heard of fancy dress took him for a bogey of the worst description and yelled with terror, in spite of the buxom cook's explaining 'It is only Master Louis inside!' So next year we went back to the Christmas tree which they knew and loved.

Quite early the fathers would come with yellow horn lanterns to guide the bairns to their cottage homes and we returned to the family fireside to laugh over the humours of the party. The winter evening ended with the children being dispatched to bed with flaring tallow candles in brass candlesticks, each with an extinguisher to suppress the objectionable smell when they were put out. The elder children remembered being sent to bed with a rush light. A long peeled rush which had been dipped in grease (the country people called them 'fried straws') was held in primitive iron pinchers, stuck in a block of wood, and it needed to be frequently pushed upward to keep it alight. A great bunch of rush lights still hung in the farmhouse attic in my childhood, and is now in Brighton Museum. White of Selborne praises them as the only means of light fit for the truly thrifty.

Peasmarsh Choir

SHEILA KAYE-SMITH

Although Sussex has been used as the setting for hundreds of popular novels – from Graham Greene's grim gangster tale, Brighton Rock, *to Stella Gibbons's parody,* Cold Comfort Farm – *Sheila Kaye-Smith is the county's only regional novelist. Her largely historical stories are set in the Weald and in the marsh country around Rye and Winchelsea. In* Sussex Gorse, *Robert, one of the sons of Reuben Backfield, a Victorian farmer near Peasmarsh, takes up carol singing.*

Robert Backfield was a member of Peasmarsh choir. He had a good, ringing bass voice, which had attracted the clerk's notice, and though Reuben disapproved of his son's having any interests outside Odiam, he realised that as a good Tory he ought to support the Church – especially as the hours of the practices did not clash with Robert's more important engagements.

Peasmarsh choir consisted of about eighteen boys and girls with an accompaniment of cornets, flutes, and a bass viol – the last played by an immensely aged drover from Coldblow, who, having only three fingers on his left hand, had to compromise, not always tunefully, with the score. The singing was erratic. Eighteen fresh young voices could not fail to give a certain pleasure, but various members had idiosyncrasies which did not make for the common weal – such as young Ditch, who never knew till he had begun to sing whether his voice would be bass or alto, all intermediary pitches being somehow unattainable – or Rosie Hubble from Barline, who was always four bars behind the rest – or even young Robert himself, who in crises of enthusiasm was wont to sing so loud that his voice drowned everyone else's, or in a wild game of follow-my-leader led the whole anthem to destruction.

Robert loved these choir practices and church singings. Though he never complained of his hard work, he was unconsciously glad of a change from the materialism of Odiam. The psalms with their outbreathings of a clearer life did much to purge even his uncultured soul of its muddlings, the hymns with their sentimental farawayness opened views into which he would gaze enchanted as into a promised land. He would come in tired and throbbing from the fields, scrape as much mud as possible off his boots, put on his Sunday coat, and tramp through the dusk to the clerk's house . . . the little golden window gleaming to him across Peasmarsh street and pond was the foretaste of the evening's sweetness.

The practices were held in the clerk's kitchen, into which the choristers would crush and huddle. On full attendance nights all elbows touched, and occasionally old Spodgram's bow would be jolted out of his hand, or someone would complain that Leacher was blowing his trumpet down his neck. Afterwards the choristers would wander home in clusters through the fields; the clusters generally split into small groups, and then the groups into couples. The couples would scatter widely, and vex their homes with late returnings.

Robert was first of all part of a cluster which included young Coalbran from Doozes, Tom Sheane from Dinglesden, the two Morfees from Edzell, Emily Ditch, and Bessie Lamb from Eggs Hole. Then in time the company reduced itself to Robert, Emily, and Bessie – and one wonderful night he found himself with Bessie alone. How they had chosen each other he

could not say. All he knew was that for some time she had become woven with the music into his thoughts. She was a poor labourer's daughter, living in a crumbled rickety cottage on Eggs Hole Farm, helping her mother look after eight young children. She was only seventeen herself, sturdy yet soft, with a mass of hay-coloured hair, and rather a broad face with wistful eyes. Robert thought she was beautiful – but Robert thought that old Spodgram's playing and the choir's singing were beautiful.

Though they were technically a Couple, they never spoke of love. They never even kissed or held each other's hands, however tenderly the velvet darkness called. He told her about his work at Odiam – about the little calf that was born that day, or the trouble he had had, patching the rent in the pigsty, or how the poultry had not taken well to their new food, but preferred something with more sharps in it. She in her turn would tell him how she had washed little Georgie's shirt – taking advantage of a warm day when he could run about naked – how her mother had lamentable hard pains all down her back, how her father had got drunk at the harvest supper and tried to beat her.

Sometimes they looked in the hedges for birds' nests, or watched the rabbits skipping in the dusk. They would gape up at the stars together and call the constellations by names of their own – Orion was 'the gurt tree,' and Cassiopeia was 'the sheep trough,' and Pegasus was 'the square meadow.'

It was all very wonderful and sweet to Robert, and when at last he crept under the sheets in the apple-smelling garret he would dream of him and Bessie wandering in the Peasmarsh fields – or. sometimes in those starry meadows where the hedges shone and twinkled with the fruit of constellations, and Charles drove his waggon along a golden road, and sheep ate from a flickering trough under a great tree of lamps.

Bessie tinted the world for Robert like a sunrise. All

Carol singers, at Soanes Farm, December 1938

through the day he carried memories of lightless woods, of fields hushed in the swale, of the smudge of her old purple cotton beside him – of, perhaps, some dim divine moment when his hand had touched hers hanging at her side.

Then winter came, with carol-singing, and the choristers tramped round, lantern-led, from farm to farm. There in the fluttering light outside Kitchenhour, Old Turk, Ellenwhorne, or Edzell, Robert would watch Bessie's chicory-flower eyes under her hood, while the steam of their breath mingled in the frosty air, and they drooped their heads together, singing to each other, only to each other, 'Good King Wenceslas,' 'As Joseph was a-walking,' or 'In the Fields with their Flocks.'

As they were both simple souls, their love only made the words more real. Sometimes it seemed almost as if they could see up in the white glistering field behind the barn, the manger with the baby in it, the mother watching near, and the ox and the ass standing meekly beside them in the straw. Bessie said she felt sure that the shepherds watched their flocks by night in the little old meadow at the corner of Totease . . . she once thought she had heard them singing. But she would not go and look.

Beef Club Drawin'

TICKNER EDWARDES

Like several more famous rural writers, Tickner Edwardes was the classic townsman-turned-countryman. A Londoner, he rejected a career in his father's firm to live in the remote village of Burpham, in the beautiful lower Arun valley, while earning his living by writing articles on country life. A keen gardener and naturalist, he mastered the art of bee-keeping and wrote two fine books, The Bee Master of Warrilow *(1907) and* The Lore of the Honey Bee *(1908), on the subject. He also wrote novels, of which* Tansy, *set in the villages of Burpham, Amberley and North Stoke was a popular success. My own favourites, however, are his accounts of rural life, of which* Neighbourhood *(1911) is the best. The book is subtitled, 'A Year's Life in and about an English Village'. The village, 'Windlecombe', is, of course, his beloved Burpham, where the Christmas Club draw is in progress.*

From the village store I moved on presently to the little sweetstuff shop, and stood awhile looking in through the holly-garlanded door. Susan sat in a wilderness of scalloped silver paper, presiding over a lucky tub. There was no getting near her to-night for the mob of children that surrounded her, and overflowed into the street; but she bawled me an affectionate Christmas greeting, and passed me, by half a dozen intervening hands – in exchange for a thrown halfpenny – a packet from the lucky-dip, which proved to contain a cherubim modelled out of pink scented soap. With this symbolic testimony to our old-time friendship bulging my pocket, I went rambling on again, and in course of time arrived at the Three Thatchers Inn. A tilt-cart was just driving away from the door. A numerous company was gathered outside, speeding the vehicle on its way with laugh and jest.

'Ye've not fared so bad,' roared old Daniel Dray, as he spied me in the darkness, 'though ye didn't come to th' drawin'. Ye've got a topside, an' a hand o' pig-meat. Stall'ard here, he's got wan o' th' turkeys, an' young George Artlett th' tother. A good club it ha' been, considerin'. An' now the lot o' us ha' got to bide here 'til Dan'l gets hoame from Stavisham wi' th' tack.'

This annual prize-drawing, and division of the Christmas Club funds, with the subsequent wait in the cosy inn parlour while the things were fetched from the town, was a great event in Windlecombe. On this one night in the year, we cultivated as a fine art the pleasure of anticipation, and each did his best to make the time go with mirth and neighbourly good-will. The occasion was also, in some degree, a kind of benefit for the landlord, to which all might contribute as a duty, if by any chance the inclination lacked. Looking round the crowded room, I could think of hardly one of the well-known faces that was missing. The old ferryman was there – how he got there was a mystery; but there he was, in the corner of the settle whence he had been absent so long. Even George Artlett had stayed to await the arrival of his turkey, and now sat at my side quaffing lemonade, his face as grave and thoughtful as ever, but his eyes twinkling with a jollity I had never seen in them before.

Young Daniel knew that no one would desire to curtail this part of the prize-drawing ceremony, and there was little fear of his wheels being heard in the sloppy street for a good two

hours to come. We stretched out our legs to the cheery blaze, and felt that for once we had succeeded in wing-clipping old Father Time.

'Beef-club drawin' agen, Dan'l!'

'Ay! beef-club drawin' agen, Tom.'

In a break in the general clamour, the two veterans exchanged the thought slowly and pensively, looking down their long pipe-stems into the fire.

'An' no one gone, Dan'l.'

'Ne'er a wan, Tom, thank God.'

'How quirk 'a do hould hisself, to be sure,' said old Tom Clemmer after a pause, and none doubted who he meant. 'Ah! an' how 'a do brisk along still! Another year o' him by – 'tis another blessin'. Here's to un, wi' all our love an' dooty!'

It was a silent toast, but drunk deep. George Artlett's glass was lighter than any when he set it down.

'But 'tain't been allers so,' old Clemmer went on ruminatively. 'How many drawin's ha' ye seen, Dan'l, boy an' man? – threescore belike, and I bean't fur ahent ye. An' many's th' time as summun's money ha' laid on th' table wi' only widder or poor-box to claim it; an' he, poor soul, quiet i' th' litten-yard up there. Ay! 'tis a lucky drawin' wi' nane but livin' hands to draw.'

Daniel Dray took up the prize-list and scanned it curiously, his white head thrown back, his spectacles straddling the extreme tip of his nose.

'An' what,' said he, 'will a single man, on-married, do wi' a whole gurt turkey-burd? An' him wi' never a wife! 'Tis wicked waste, neighbours! Him an' th' parrot, they'll ha' nought but turkey-meat i' th' house from now to Lady-time.'

Stallwood's beady black eyes disappeared in a wide smile.

'I knowed a man once,' he said, 'out in Utah State in Murriky, 'twur – as got a brace o' ostriches at a Christmas drawin'; an' when it come to carvin' at dinner-time, th' pore

Free range turkeys at Mr W.R. Caine's farm at Frant, 1934

feller, he got no more 'n half a bite fer hisself because—' He stopped, suddenly recollecting George Artlett's lustrating presence, 'Ah! he wur married, I tell ye, an' never a wured o' a lie!'

'What'll 'a do wi' it, Dan'l?' The old ferryman leant from his corner eagerly, staring at the wall as though he saw there the picture that rose in his mind. 'What'll 'a do wi' it? Jest think o't! Nobbut hisself in a quiet kitchen o' Christmas morning – his boots on, an' nane to rate un for spannellin' about – click-clack from the roastin' Jack, an' tick-tack from th' clock, an' a good cuss now an' agen from th' ould parrot, but never a wured o' wimmin's wrath. Ah, life! – 'tis all jest a gurt beef-club drawin'! Some on us draws peace an' quiet an' turkey-burds, an' some draws—'

His lips closed on his pipe-stem with a snap. A commiserate shake of the head went round the company.

'An' here,' went on old Daniel, still conning the prize-list, 'here be Jack Farley wi' bare money an' fower ounces o'

tobacker – him as doan't smoke, an' has sixteen i' family. Lor', Jack! how that there deuce-ace do foller ye i' life!'

Jack Farley sat in the draughtiest seat by the door, his invariable modest choice of station. No one had ever seen him without a smile on his emaciated, sun-blackened face; and now he was smiling more determinedly than ever.

'I dunno', Dan'l,' he expostulated gently. ''Twur a real double-six when 'er an' me come together all they years ago. An' th' chillern, they be good throws, every wan. An' that there noo little 'un, Dan'l – nauthin' o' th' deuce-ace about him, I tell ye! But them as putts to sea, Dan'l, thcy must look fer rough weather, time and agen.'

He squared himself and gazed about him as though his weekly carter-wage of fourteen shillings were as many pounds. Then he beat his mug upon the table jovially. 'An' now,' said he, 'I'll sing ye 'Th' Mistletoe Bough!''

It was the beginning of the real entertainment of the evening. Vocal music in the Three Thatchers at ordinary times was accounted a rather disreputable thing – a mere tap-room vulgarism – by the habitual parlour company; but on certain rare nights in the year, of which this was one, every man present was expected to sing. One by one now, in Jack Farley's wake, followed the rest of the assembly, and every song had a chorus that shook the very roof-beams of the house. No man thought of looking at the clock until, in the midst of a doleful melody from the landlord, old Tom Clemmer suddenly sprang to his one available foot.

''Tis th' cart!' he cried, and made for the door. In the general stampede after him, I heard Captain Stallwood's grumbling voice:

'Ut bean't right nohow fer people as caan't use tobacker to draw un away from them as can. I means to ha' that there fower ounces, Dan'l. An' Jack Farley – th' ould swab! – 'a must make out as best 'a can wi' th' turkey-burd.'

A Medieval Legend of Winchelsea

WILLIAM AXON

A Monkish scribe of the thirteenth century has left us a Latin version of a curious tradition of bygone Sussex. According to this chronicler there was once an avaricious man living in the neighbourhood of Winchelsea, who hoarded in a chest money which was of no benefit either to himself or to others. One day, as he went to look at his beloved treasure, he saw sitting on the box a little black demon. If he was startled at the sight, he was still more startled to hear this apparition exclaim, 'Begone, this money is not thine; it belongs to Godwin, the Smith.' Unable to make use of the treasure himself, he decided that no one else should have it. He therefore hollowed out the trunk of a great tree, put the box in it, closed up the ends, and threw it into the sea. The waters carried the trunk to the door of Godwin, who dwelt in the next town – evidently Rye. Godwin who was a righteous and innocent man was preparing to hold a Christmas festival, and the appearance of this log was a source of rejoicing, as it would evidently make a capital yule log. So the Smith carried home the tree trunk, and put it in his fireplace. On Christmas Eve the fire was lighted, and the heat caused the money within the box to melt and the metal ran out. Godwin's wife saw this, and taking the log from the fire, she hid it. The result was that Godwin the Smith became rich, whilst the Winchelsea man was forced to beg his bread from door to door. But the story of the manner in which the miser had lost his wealth became known, and when he begged at the Smith's house, the wife of Godwin thought she would give the poor caitiff some help. So one day she baked a loaf, and hid forty shillings in it, and gave it to the beggar. The miser went his way, and soon after met some fishermen on the beach to whom he sold the loaf unbroken, for a penny. The fishermen came to Godwin's house, and were about to give the loaf to their horses when the mistress recognized it, and let them have some oats instead. So the miser remained poor to the end of his days.

Duncton village Christmas party in January 1948

Eddi's Service

RUDYARD KIPLING

If imperial India was Kipling's first inspiration as a writer, then the Sussex countryside was surely his second. In 1897, his Raj days over, he settled, first in the little farming village of Rottingdean and then, five years later, at Burwash in the Weald. It was while he was living at Burwash that he wrote two of his most enchanting books for children, Puck of Pook's Hill *and* Rewards and Fairies, *which include some of his most memorable Sussex verses such as 'The Run of the Downs' and 'The Way through the Woods'. One of my own favourites is 'Eddi's Service', preface to the chapter on St Wilfred whom legend credits with the conversion of Saxon Sussex.*

Eddi, priest of St. Wilfrid
  In the chapel at Manhood End,
Ordered a midnight service
  For such as cared to attend.

But the Saxons were keeping Christmas,
  And the night was stormy as well.
Nobody came to service
  Though Eddi rang the bell.

'Wicked weather for walking,'
  Said Eddi of Manhood End.

'But I must go on with the service
For such as care to attend.'

The altar candles were lighted, –
An old marsh donkey came,
Bold as a guest invited,
And stared at the guttering flame.

The storm beat on at the windows,
The water splashed on the floor,
And a wet yoke-weary bullock
Pushed in through the open door.

'How do I know what is greatest,
How do I know what is least?
That is My Father's business,'
Said Eddi, Wilfrid's priest.

'But, three are gathered together –
Listen to me and attend.
I bring good news my brethren!'
Said Eddi, of Manhood End.

And he told the Ox of a manger
And a stall in Bethlehem,
And he spoke to the Ass of a Rider
That rode to Jerusalem.

They steamed and dripped in the chancel,
They listened and never stirred,
While, just as though they were Bishops,
Eddi preached them The Word.

Till the gale blew off on the marshes
  And the windows showed the day,
And the Ox and ass together
  Wheeled and clattered away.

And when the Saxons mocked him,
  Said Eddi of Manhood End,
'I dare not shut His chapel
  On such as care to attend.'

Bethlehem at Berwick

ELIZABETH ROBERTS

Wherever you may be on Christmas Eve, come with me, if you will, in mind and spirit, to the beautiful little downland church of St Michael and All Angels at Berwick.

We must start from Seaford at an hour before midnight, and take the road leading to High-and-Over. If there is a moon, we may get a glimpse of Cuckmere Haven and the lazy river meandering through the valley beneath us on its way to the sea. Then downhill we speed, braking sharply at the hairpin bends, before climbing West Hill through over-hanging trees. Very soon we approach that charming village of Alfriston and,

slowing down, we make our way up the quaint street, past the Star Inn and the Market Cross.

Just another mile or two along the narrow, winding lanes of the Cuckmere valley, and we arrive at our destination. Berwick, unlike her neighbour Alfriston, is very wide awake, and ready to welcome the small bands of motorists, cyclists, and pedestrians who come, year by year, to take part in the Midnight Service. Tonight the ground in front of the Rectory is used as a car park, but there will be neither jostling nor noisy chatter, for we who gather at Berwick on Christmas Eve are of one mind and purpose. We come to welcome and to worship the Christ Child.

Aided by torches, we stumble along the rough and muddy path from the Rectory, climb some rather slippery stone steps under an archway of trees, and then straight before us, its tall steeple seeming to touch the heavens, stands the brilliantly lighted church.

We must enter by the north door, but first, in case you are a stranger to these parts, I must prepare you for a surprise. During recent years, Sussex artists have been busily engaged in covering the white-washed walls with colourful mural paintings. The principal murals represent Christ in Glory, over the chancel arch, by Duncan Grant, an Annunciation and Nativity, on the south and north walls, by Vanessa Bell – sister of Virginia Woolf – and the Wise and Foolish Virgins by Quentin Bell. Paintings of the saints surround the pulpit, and in the panelling of the screen are country scenes depicting the four seasons of the year. Some declare the murals distracting, and cling to the Reformation legacy of unadorned churches. For myself, I cannot but find St Michael's charming.

The whole church is a blaze of light. There are candles everywhere; tall ones on the altar, tiny ones above the screen and on the window ledges and in the chancel stands a Christmas tree, brilliantly illuminated. We find seats on the

right of the aisle. Already we begin to forget ourselves, our cares and anxieties, grievances and petty jealousies, for we have entered into the spirit of Christmas.

The organist settles herself and begins to coax festive music from the ornate and antiquated instrument. Until just over a year ago, the village children took turns in acting as organ blower, but now electricity has deprived them of this task.

Suddenly the bell ceases to clang, and the last straggler hurriedly finds a vacant seat. Slowly the servers enter the church from the vestry on the north side of the sanctuary, followed by the priest clothed in a magnificent cope. We stand for the processional hymn, while servers and priest wend their way down the south aisle to the tower, where the crib has been set. There is silence while this symbol of Christmastide is blessed with holy water and then, as the tiny procession makes its way back to the sanctuary, we continue our hymn.

'O God, who has made this most sacred night to shine with the brightness of the true light . . .' begins the priest, and we live again the first Christmas. Glancing across at the north wall we see the painting of the Nativity. The Blessed Virgin holds the Child Jesus while St Joseph, the shepherds, the ox and the ass, and some Berwick children gaze with adoration. The stable door stands open, and in the background are painted the glorious Downs which stand sentinel over Berwick.

Here in the heart of the English countryside, surrounded by kindly village folk, we join with all Christians everywhere in greeting the new-born King. In nearby barns and fields are horses and cattle, dogs and sheep, and we remember the story of the animals who knelt at this hour of midnight to offer their humble adoration.

All too soon the service is over and we must leave St Michael's and journey home. But, truly, we have visited Bethlehem, and there, amidst peace and felicity, offered our

praise and thanks. As we go out into the night, the words of an ancient carol are on our lips:

> Join then all hearts that are not stone,
> And all our voices prove,
> To celebrate this holy One.
> The God of peace and love.

Christmas Greetings

E.F. BENSON

Even today Rye has kept much of its pre-war charm: a place of literary ghosts, narrow, cobbled and seemingly timeless streets, old smuggling inns, beautiful houses and, in the weeks before Christmas, of tantalizing, misty views over the Sussex marshes. It is also a safe haven for the eccentric.

Benson's comic novels of Rye life during the 1920s and the 1930s are today as fresh, as funny, and as indispensable as then. Mapp and Lucia *is the fourth in the ever-popular Lucia novels – the one which brings Lucia, fresh from her dramatic triumph at the Elizabethan fete at Riseholme, to the small country town of*

Tilling (Benson's name for Rye). With her, and firmly in tow, is her friend and aide-de-camp, Georgie Pillson. These nouveau arrivés *are at first welcomed by Elizabeth Mapp, whose house ('Mallards') Lucia rents for the summer season. But when Lucia decides to sell Riseholme and move to Tilling, Miss Mapp feels her position as queen-bee of Tilling society under threat. The result is an hilarious and undeclared 'war' in which bridge parties, art exhibitions, and dinner invitations are but the minor engagements of a long-fought campaign, as Miss Mapp tries (unsuccessfully) to enlist the support of her friend Diva and other Tillingites against the newcomers. As Christmas approaches, it seems that there may be a truce for the season of goodwill.*

The pleasant custom of sending Christmas cards prevailed in Tilling, and most of the world met in the stationer's shop on Christmas Eve, selecting suitable salutations from the three-penny, the sixpenny and shilling trays. Elizabeth came in rather early and had almost completed her purchases when some of her friends arrived, and she hung about looking at the backs of volumes in the lending-library, but keeping an eye on what they purchased. Diva, she observed, selected nothing from the shilling tray any more than she had herself; in fact, she thought that Diva's purchases this year were made entirely from the threepenny tray. Susan, on the other hand, ignored the threepenny tray and hovered between the sixpennies and the shillings and expressed an odiously opulent regret that there were not some 'choicer' cards to be obtained. The Padre and Mrs Bartlett were certainly exclusively threepenny, but that was always the case. However they, like everybody else, studied the other trays, so that when, next morning, they all received seasonable coloured greetings from their friends, a person must have a shocking memory if he did not know what

Christmas card, 1936, by Harold Roberts, photographed by George Garland

had been the precise cost of all that were sent him. But Georgie and Lucia as was universally noticed, though without comment, had not been in at all, in spite of the fact that they had been seen about in the High Street together and going into other shops. Elizabeth therefore decided that they did not intend to send any Christmas cards and before paying for what she had chosen, she replaced in the threepenny tray a pretty picture of a robin sitting on a sprig of mistletoe which she had meant to send Georgie. There was no need to put back what she had chosen for Lucia, since the case did not arise.

Christmas Day dawned, a stormy morning with a strong gale from the south-west, and on Elizabeth's breakfast-table was a pile of letters, which she tore open. Most of them were threepenny Christmas cards, a sixpenny from Susan, smelling of musk, and none from Lucia or Georgie. She had anticipated that, and it was pleasant to think that she had put back into the threepenny tray the one she had selected for him, before purchasing it.

The rest of her post was bills, some of which must be stoutly disputed when Christmas was over, and she found it difficult to realize the jollity appropriate to the day. Last evening various choirs of amateur riffraffs and shrill bobtails had rendered the night hideous by repetitions of 'Good King Wenceslas' and 'The First Noël', church-bells borne on squalls of wind and rain had awakened her while it was still dark and now sprigs of holly kept falling down from the picture-frames where Withers had perched them. Bacon made her feel rather better, and she went to church, with a mackintosh against these driving gusts of rain, and a slightly blue nose against this boisterous wind. Diva was coming to a dinner-lunch: this was an annual institution held at Wasters and Mallards alternately.

Elizabeth hurried out of church at the conclusion of the service by a side door, not feeling equal to joining in the gay group of her friends who with Lucia as their centre were

Christmas card, 1936, by Harold Roberts, photographed by George Garland

gathered at the main entrance. The wind was stronger than ever, but the rain had ceased and she battled her way round the square surrounding the church before she went home. Close to Mallards Cottage she met Georgie holding his hat on against the gale. He wished her a merry Christmas, but then his hat had been whisked off his head; something very strange happened to his hair, which seemed to have been blown off his skull, leaving a quite bare place there, and he vanished in frenzied pursuit of his hat with long tresses grown from the side of his head streaming in the wind. A violent draught eddying round the corner by the garden-room propelled her into Mallards holding on to the knocker, and it was with difficulty that she closed the door. On the table in the hall stood a substantial package, which had certainly not been there when she left. Within its wrappings was a *terrine of pâté de foie gras* with a most distinguished label on it, and a card fluttered on to the floor, proclaiming that wishes for a merry Christmas from Lucia and Georgie accompanied it. Elizabeth instantly conquered the feeble temptation of sending this gift back again in the manner in which she had returned that basket of tomatoes from her own garden. Tomatoes were not *pâté*. But what a treat for Diva!

Diva arrived, and they went straight in to the banquet. The *terrine* was wrapped in a napkin, and Withers handed it to Diva. She helped herself handsomely to the truffles and the liver.

'How delicious!' she said. 'And such a monster!'

'I hope it's good,' said Elizabeth, not mentioning the donors. 'It ought to be. Paris.'

Diva suddenly caught sight of a small label pasted below the distinguished one. It was that of the Tilling grocer, and a flood of light poured in upon her.

'Lucia and Mr Georgie have sent such lovely Christmas presents to everybody,' she said. 'I felt quite ashamed of myself for only having given them threepenny cards.'

'How sweet of them,' said Elizabeth. 'What were they?'

'A beautiful box of hard chocolates for me,' said Diva. 'And a great pot of caviare for Susan, and an umbrella for the Padre – his blew inside out in the wind yesterday – and—'

'And this beautiful *pâté* for me,' interrupted Elizabeth, grasping the nettle, for it was obvious that Diva had guessed. 'I was just going to tell you.'

Diva knew that was a lie, but it was no use telling Elizabeth so, because she knew it too, and she tactfully changed the subject.

'I shall have to do my exercises three times to-day after such a lovely lunch,' she said, as Elizabeth began slicing the turkey. But that was not a well-chosen topic, for subjects connected with Lucia might easily give rise to discord and she tried again and again and again, bumping, in her spinning-top manner, from one impediment to another.

'Major Benjy can play the scale of C with his right hand' – (No, that wouldn't do). 'What an odd voice Susan's got: she sang an Italian song the other day at' – (Worse and worse). 'I sent two pictures to the winter exhibition' – (Worse if possible: there seemed to be no safe topic under the sun). 'A terrific gale, isn't it? There'll be three days of tremendous high tides for the wind is heaping them up. I should not wonder if the road by Grebe—' (she gave it up: it was no use) – 'isn't flooded to-morrow.'

Elizabeth behaved like a perfect lady. She saw that Diva was doing her best to keep off disagreeable subjects on Christmas Day, but there were really no others. All topics led to Lucia.

'I hope not,' she said, 'for with all the field-paths soaked from the rain it is my regular walk just now. But not very likely, dear, for after the last time that the road was flooded, they built the bank opposite – opposite that house much higher.'

They talked for quite a long while about gales and tides and

dykes in complete tranquility. Then the proletarian diversions of Boxing Day seemed safe.

'There's a new film to-morrow at the Picture Palace about tadpoles,' said Elizabeth. 'So strange to think they become toads: or is it frogs? I think I must go.'

'Lucia's giving a Christmas-tree for the choir-boys in the evening, in that great kitchen of hers,' said Diva.

'How kind!' said Elizabeth hastily, to show she took no offence.

'And in the afternoon there's a whist drive at the Institute,' said Diva. 'I'm letting both my servants go, and Lucia's sending all hers too. I am not sure I should like to be quite alone in a house along that lonely road. We in the town could scream from a top window if burglars got into our houses and raise the alarm.'

'It would be a very horrid burglar who was so wicked on Boxing Day,' observed Elizabeth sententiously. 'Ah, here's the plum pudding! Blazing beautifully, Withers! So pretty!'

Diva became justifiably somnolent when lunch was over, and after half an hour's careful conversation she went off home to have a nice long nap, which she expressed by the word exercises. Elizabeth wrote two notes of gratitude to the donors of the *pâté* and sat herself down to think seriously of what she could do. She had refused Lucia's invitation to tea a few days before, thus declaring her attitude, and now it seemed to her that that was a mistake, for she had cut herself off from the opportunities of reprisals which intercourse with her might have provided. She had been unable, severed like this, to devise anything at all effective; all she could do was to lie awake at night hating Lucia, and this seemed to be quite barren of results. It might be better (though bitter) to join that callisthenic class in order to get a foot in the enemy's territory. Her note of thanks for the *pâté* would have paved the way towards such a step, and though it would certainly be eating humble pie to ask to join an affair that she had openly derided, it would be pie with a purpose. As it was, for a whole week she had had no opportunities, she had surrounded herself with a smoke- cloud, she heard nothing about Lucia any more, except when clumsy Diva let out things by accident. All she knew was that Lucia, busier than any bee known to science, was undoubtedly supreme in all the social activities which she herself had been accustomed to direct, and to remain, like Achilles in his tent, did not lead to anything. Also she had an idea that Tilling expected of her some exhibition of spirit and defiance, and no one was more anxious than she to fulfil those expectations to the utmost. So she settled she would go to Grebe to-morrow, and, after thanking her in person for the *pâté*, ask to join the callisthenic class. Tilling, and Lucia too, no doubt would take that as a sign of surrender, but let them wait a while, and they should see.

'I can't fight her unless I get in touch with her,' reflected Elizabeth; 'at least I don't see how, and I'm sure I've thought enough.'

From

A Country Calendar

TICKNER EDWARDES

My grandmother always spoke of cut holly as 'Christmas', and it is still called that in parts of West Sussex and Hampshire. Gathering it, together with ivy and, when lucky, mistletoe, remains one of the joys of the week before Christmas. Few of us, however, are quite so observant about holly as Tickner Edwardes.

Now and again, as I pass along, the light of the lantern just catches on the holly-berries. It is certain now that there will be no lack in English homes – or need be none, at least – of bright-berried holly for the garland-making at Christmas, and it is equally certain that many people, whose only acquaintance with holly is an indoor one at this season, will be noticing how much of its green glossy foliage is without the usual spines.

The holly's overflowing horn of plenty this December is due indirectly to the long-continued mildness of the times. When winter sets in very early, and with unusual severity, the stores of rose and may-berries on the countryside are prematurely

Holly-gathering at Upperton Common, December 1935. An old hand helps the children out. A posed picture but none the less wonderful for that

exhausted, and the birds must come to the attractive, yet ill-flavoured holly, or starve. But in seasons of mild, open weather, such as has been experienced lately – especially in good blossom years like the present – the plenitude of hips and haws, supplemented by the fact that mild winters delay the crowding of the normally insectivorous birds to the hedgerows for food, has almost wholly kept the holly-berries from depredation.

Sometimes, however, it happens that the holly will bear its scarlet load of fruit untouched till well into December. And then, the hard frosts suddenly setting in, Christmas finds the holly-berries all but gone, the garland makers bereft of their chief supplies.

The absence of prickly leaves, which will probably be observed on some of the most richly and profusely berried holly-boughs gathered for decoration this year, is explained by the circumstance that the older trees have borne exceptionally well this season on their upper branches, so well, in fact, that it has been worthwhile to climb for their treasure of densely clustered fruit.

If the holly is not a tree that thinks, it is not easy to understand its plan of life in regard to this question of spined and unspined foliage.

The whole plant – bark and leaf and tender twig – is good to eat, as most four-footed creatures know. The young holly saplings have a perilous time of it in natural, unprotected situations, not a tithe of them ever reaching maturity. But where one has chanced to attain such girth and height as to defy the bark-nibbling rabbits it is only to find itself beset with new dangers. Browsing animals would soon strip it of its fleshy, succulent leaves if it did not put on this formidable armament of prickles.

Yet – and here is where the holly-tree seems to make a reasonable proposition of life as opposed to an instinctive one –

it grows these prickly defences only to the height normally reached by its larger hungry foes. Above that line the leaves swiftly lose their sharp, strong barbs, and the upper regions of growth bear only smooth, unspined foliage, though there the brilliant-hued berries make a braver show than ever.

Christmas Day

ANDREW YOUNG

Although Andrew Young, for many years the Vicar of Stonegate (near Burwash), is today most widely appreciated for his fine nature poems, he also wrote some of the best religious verse in English this century.

Last night in the open shippen*
   The Infant Jesus lay
While cows stood at the hay-crib
   Twitching the sweet hay.

As I trudged through the snow-fields
   That lay in their own light,
A thorn-bush with its shadow
   Stood doubled on the night.

And I stayed on my journey
   To listen to the cheep

* Shippen: (dialect) byre, cowshed.

Bayleaf, a restored timber-frame house, at the Open Air Museum, Singleton

Of a small bird in the thorn-bush
  I woke from its puffed sleep.

The bright stars were my angels
  And with the heavenly host
I sang praise to the Father,
  The Son and Holy Ghost.

Christmas Bells

THOMAS GEERING

The sweet sound of bells ringing out over the home fields is still one of the joys of Christmas morn. Here Thomas Geering, the chronicler of Hailsham, reminisces about the churchbell ringers in the early eighteenth century. Geering was born in 1813 and his book, originally called Our Parish, A Medley; By One who has never lived out of it, *was published in 1884.*

Again looking back, we may note a few other features and changes. To begin with our church ringers. Then the master tradesman thought it no degradation, but rather an honourable distinction, to be the one to minister to the rights of the belfry. To be a ringer was a privilege. I remember but one new hand, and he carried his election by force of prescriptive right and family interest. His father had been one of the fraternity, and a brother stood then foremost man as leader. Each bell had its regular hand. There was the hatter, glover, tailor, shoemaker, and blacksmith in succession, and a few others – odd men to take a turn as occasion required, and one, the street driver, who was always needed to fetch the beer from the tavern. They were all professionally earnest, devoted men, and to do them justice, as a rule – and what rule is not more or less broken? -- they were sober men. But the potent god, bred of malt and hops, at times got possession of the brain, and then was the time to take note of the work of the features and lips as the ropes flew up and down.

On practice nights and rare occasions they would treat the outside world with a set of changes. Four bells allowed but little variation, yet with the steady and even pull of the tenor by the tall blacksmith, George Huggett, and the clear, unerring lead of the hatter, Samuel Jenner, the old-fashioned peal was considered to be eclipsed by the change of four-and-twenty.

The great treat of the year was, when I was a boy, to be awakened on Christmas morning by the early clatter of the bells, and to lay awake watching until midnight on New Year's eve to hear the old year rung out and the new year rung in; and during the whole of my life I have never once upon these occasions been beyond the reach of the gladdening sound. I have hoped to live to hear a fuller peal. I have importuned those in authority upon the subject, but with no success, to add a sixth. Our old ringers would yearly make a house-to-house call, and accept any gratuity as an acknow-ledgement for their services. What master tradesman now among us would do the like?

The Shepherd's Christmas

BARCLAY WILLS

Most of us like to see friends at Christmas, and Barclay Wills chose to visit one or other of the old Downland shepherds he knew so well. In 1923, while living in Brighton, he tramped out on to the Downs beyond Falmer, to Mary Farm, where Nelson Coppard was to be found at work with his sheep. It was there some years before, during one of his rambles over the hills, that Barclay had chanced upon Nelson in a little valley by the farm. The two men took to each other at once, as Barclay recalled in his classic book, Shepherds of Sussex:

'He was the first shepherd I ever met. From him I had my first instruction on sheep-bells, crooks, and the details of a shepherd's life. To the lucky natives of Sussex a meeting with a shepherd is just an ordinary incident in a Downland ramble, but to a Londoner, blessed with an artistic temperament, that first sudden entry into a little valley full of sheep with their ancient bells chiming, the meeting with a jovial shepherd with his glittering crook, the chat with him, and the return journey, when I carried home wild flowers and two large canister bells, was overwhelming. I felt that I had stepped into a new world.'

Barclay Wills' sensitive study of a robin. A preparatory sketch, drawn from life, on tracing paper. It was Barclay's custom to send friends Christmas cards with one of his published bird illustrations on. Often he would also sketch a small bird, such as his 'favourite' the wren, on the back of the envelope

Few people expect to go to their ordinary work on Christmas Day, and fewer still on every one of the other three hundred and sixty-four days also; yet this is the record of a certain Downland shepherd, and he does it without grumbling.

He will not be at home for a merry dinner-party at midday, but his grandchildren will welcome him at tea-time when his work is done. A week ago he said to me: 'Come Christmas Day I'll be right over t' brow yonder. Goo home to dinner? No, I wun't; 'tis too far there an' back agin. Reckon I sh'd be middlin' hungry time I got back to team, an' want 'nother dinner! I bean't so young as I was. One time I ran up an' down t' old hills like doin' nothin', but now I goes slower. I be like t' old bell yokes – they doos their work an' they be tough, but they wears an' wears till they breaks asunder – an' I be wearin'!'

Should the day be fine, my friend will eat his frugal lunch in the open, with his dog for company, and the sheep bells will provide the music he loves best. Last Christmas, to my surprise, he made me a present of his favourite big bell. Pleased as I was to accept it, the fact remains that a bell was the only thing he had to give, and he gave the best he owned. How few of us would willingly offer our most cherished possession to a friend as a Christmas gift!

The shepherd gets no stone of beef at Christmas as he did in the old days when Sussex farms were worked by Sussex farmers. He can recall his enjoyment of these days – of harvest suppers, of little remembrances at lambing time and shearing time.

Sometimes, in course of conversation, I obtain a glimpse of the sturdy, independent character of the old Downsman. He is a man of simple faith, who would stand against a hundred others for his opinion, and would work like a slave from a sense of duty; a man who will give away his favourite possession, who will point out the beauty of a wild flower, and go to any trouble to prevent one of his flock from wearing an uncom-

'My friend the shepherd.' Barclay Wills' loving portrait, taken with his Box Brownie, of Nelson Coppard, the first and closest of his shepherd friends

fortable bell-collar. Perhaps his life of unending work among the beauties of nature has caused him to view life from a different standpoint from ours, but his quaintly expressed opinions are often equal to the cream of a church sermon.

Should you have a spare hour or two at this season of peace and goodwill, and you know of a shepherd of the old school, it will refresh you to tread the Downland paths, where peace reigns, and to hear the gentle song of the old bells. Before you start, remember that the figure with the crook is very human, and put some tobacco in your pocket for the old man on the hill.

* * *

This is not the end of this story. Nelson's Christmas gift, complete with its original tackle of wooden yoke, lockyers, and bell straps still exists. Tied to it are two old-fashioned shop labels, testifying in Barclay's beautiful pencil handwriting that this was 'Nelson Coppard's favourite bell'! With the bell is a two page manuscript, in Barclay's hand, giving its history:

Nelson's favourite Canister Bell
last used at Mary Farm, Falmer, 1925

Height $5\frac{1}{2}$ inches
Crown $4\frac{1}{4} \times 3\frac{1}{4}$
Weight (without tackle) 1 lb 14 ozs

This is a fine typical specimen canister, in excellent condition, although worn in staples, crown ring, tongue, and rim. It belonged to Nelson Coppard. He heard it for the first time about the year 1875, when it was owned by a young shepherd of Hangleton near Devil's Dyke. He took a great fancy to it and purchased it for 1s 6d. It was not new when he bought it. Years afterwards, when at Iford he parted with it, but soon bought it back again and it remained his favourite 'big 'un'.

As related above, he presented it to me at Christmas 1923, much to my surprise. Many times we had listened to its song when on the hills together, and I could guess what it meant to him to part with it. At a later date I asked him if he missed its company, and as he reluctantly admitted that he did I asked him to use it again on the understanding that it was still mine. To this he agreed, and once more its deep note sounded on the Falmer–Plumpton hills.

How a Sussex Christmas Should Be Kept

HILAIRE BELLOC

A Sussex shepherd told Barclay Wills, 'My gran'father did it thet way, an' my father did it thet way, an' now I *doos it the same. There be a right way an' a wrong way o' doin' things, an' the sooner you learns to do a thing the right way the better it be for ye . . .'* Shepherds of Sussex.

This sentiment would surely have appealed to Hilaire

· A Sussex Christmas ·

Belloc, to whom the old ways of rural Sussex were precious. His essay, 'A Remaining Christmas', published in 1928, from which this piece comes, depicts a Christmas celebration at home in Sussex. In the opening passage, which is omitted, Belloc describes his home at Shipley, stressing its warmth and local character. It was a house, part ancient, part Victorian – of oak beams and open hearths, in which 'wood only' was burnt, 'and that wood oak'. There was no electric light, which Belloc hated, and the place was lit with candles and oil lamps. So his was Christmas by candle-light; unhurried, simple, joyful, a celebration of peace.

On Christmas Eve a great quantity of holly and of laurel is brought in from the garden and from the farm (for this house has a farm of a hundred acres attached to it and an oak wood of ten acres). This greenery is put up all over the house in every room just before it becomes dark on that day. Then there is brought into the hall a young pine tree, about twice the height of a man, to serve for a Christmas tree, and on this innumerable little candles are fixed, and presents for all the household and the guests and the children of the village.

It is about five o'clock that these last come into the house, and at that hour in England, at that date, it has long been quite dark; so they come into a house all illuminated with the Christmas tree shining like a cluster of many stars seen through a glass.

The first thing done after the entry of these people from the village and their children (the children are in number about fifty – for this remote place keeps a good level through the generations and does not shrink or grow, but remains itself) is a common meal, where all eat and drink their fill in the offices. Then the children come in to the Christmas tree. They are each given a silver piece one by one, and one by one, their presents.

'Christmas Story': one of Garland's most charming pictures which captures the magic that Christmas and stories have always had for country children. Ghost stories were once a popular pastime at Christmas in Sussex before the advent of television, but Garland's title suggests that the narrative which enthralls the children is the Christmas story itself

After that they dance in the hall and sing songs, which have been handed down to them for I do not know how long. These songs are game-songs, and are sung to keep time with the various parts in each game, and the men and things and animals which you hear mentioned in these songs are all of that countryside. Indeed, the tradition of Christmas here is what it should be everywhere, knit into the very stuff of the place; so that I fancy the little children, when they think of Bethlehem, see it in their minds as though it were in the winter depth of England, which is as it should be.

These games and songs continue for as long as they will, and then they file out past the great fire in the hearth to a

small piece adjoining where a crib has been set up with images of Our Lady and St Joseph and the Holy Child, the shepherds, and what I will call, by your leave, the Holy animals. And here, again, tradition is so strong in this house that these figures are never new-bought, but are as old as the oldest of the children of the family, now with children of their own. On this account, the donkey has lost one of its plaster ears, and the old ox which used to be all brown is now piebald, and of the shepherds, one actually has no head. But all that is lacking is imagined. There hangs from the roof of the crib over the Holy Child a tinsel star grown rather obscure after all these years, and much too large for the place. Before this crib the children (some of them Catholic and some Protestant, for the village is mixed) sing their carols; the one they know best is the one which begins: 'The First good Joy that Mary had, it was the joy of One.' There are a half a dozen or so of these carols which the children here sing; and mixed with their voices is the voice of the miller (for this house has a great windmill attached to it). The miller is famous in these parts for his singing, having a very deep and loud voice which is his pride. When these carols are over, all disperse, except those who are living in the house, but the older ones are not allowed to go without more good drink for their viaticum, a sustenance for Christian men.

Then the people of the house, when they have dined, and their guests, with the priest who is to say Mass for them, sit up till near midnight. There is brought in a very large log of oak (you must be getting tired of oak by this time! But everything here is oaken, for the house is of the Weald). This log of oak is the Christmas or Yule log and the rule is that it must be too heavy for one man to lift; so two men come, bringing it in from outside, the master of the house and his servant. They cast it down upon the fire in the great hearth of the dining-room, and the superstition is that, if it burns all night and is found still smouldering in the morning, the home will be prosperous for the coming year.

With that they all go up to the chapel and there the three night Masses are said, one after the other, and those of the household take their Communion.

Next morning they sleep late, and the great Christmas dinner is at midday. It is a turkey; and a plum pudding, with holly in it and everything conventional, and therefore satisfactory, is done. Crackers are pulled, the brandy is lit and poured over the pudding till the holly crackles in the flame and the curtains are drawn a moment that the flames may be seen. This Christmas feast, so great that it may be said almost to fill the day, they may reprove who will; but for my part I applaud.

Now, you must not think that Christmas being over, the season and its glories are at an end, for in this house there is kept up the full custom of the Twelve Days, so that 'Twelfth Day', the Epiphany, still has, to its inhabitants, its full and ancient meaning as it had when Shakespeare wrote. The green is kept in its place in every room, and not a leaf of it must be moved until Epiphany morning, but on the other hand not a leaf of it must remain in the house, nor the Christmas tree either, by Epiphany evening. It is all taken out and burnt in a special little coppice reserved for these good trees which have done their Christmas duty; and now, after so many years, you might almost call it a little forest, for each tree has lived, bearing witness to the holy vitality of unbroken ritual and inherited things.

In the midst of this season between Christmas and Twelfth Day comes the ceremony of the New Year, and this is how it is observed.

On New Year's Eve, at about a quarter to twelve o'clock at night, the master of the house and all that are with him go about from room to room opening every door and window, however cold the weather be, for thus, they say, the old year

and its burdens can go out and leave everything new for hope and for the youth of the coming time.

This also is a superstition, and of the best. Those who observe it trust that it is as old as Europe, and with roots stretching back into forgotten times.

While this is going on the bells in the church hard by are ringing out the old year, and when all the windows and doors have thus been opened and left wide, all those in the house go outside, listening for the cessation of the chimes, which comes just before the turn of the year. There is an odd silence of a few

A cut-out card in the shape of an ivy leaf, *c.* 1885. Ivy was then still used in country homes as Christmas decoration along with the holly and mistletoe

minutes, and watches are consulted to make certain of the time (for this house detests wireless and has not even a telephone), and the way they know the moment of midnight is by the boom of a gun, which is fired at a town far off, but can always be heard.

At that sound the bells of the church clash out suddenly in new chords, the master of the house goes back into it with a piece of stone or earth from outside, all doors are shut, and the household, all of them, rich and poor, drink a glass of wine together to salute the New Year.

This, which I have just described, is not in a novel or a play. It is real, and goes on as the ordinary habit of living men and women. I fear that set down thus in our terribly changing time it must sound very strange and, perhaps in places, grotesque, but to those who practise it, it is not only sacred, but normal, having in the whole of the complicated affair a sacramental quality and an effect of benediction; not to be despised.

Indeed, modern men, who lack such things, lack sustenance, and our fathers who founded all those ritual observances were very wise.

Thin Ice

BOB COPPER

Christmas is nothing without mirth and Bob Copper, whose books are well salted with dry country wit, can be trusted to provide it. I've re-read this passage from his third book Early to Rise *(subtitled 'A Sussex Boyhood') many times and still it makes me chuckle!*

The job of taking the Christmas dinner down to the bake-house at the back of the Black Horse had been passed down a generation to Ron and me, and at about half-past seven we would set off with our precious load. We still had a huge round of beef every year, although it was no longer a present from the farmer as it had been in Grand-dad's day, and for the convenience of carving this and the large turkey, together with an enamel dinner-can with a tight-fitting lid in which to bring home the dripping, Dad had made a wooden carrier like a stretcher about six feet long with two handles at each end. The bird and the joint, thickly daubed with dripping, would be covered with grease-proof paper, then with several layers of clean corn sacks to keep in the heat on the return journey and finally draped with a white linen table cloth.

As we walked down to the village and turned into the almost deserted High Street, the funereal appearance of our burden would prompt suitable quips from the one or two men we did see. 'Let's 'ave a look at the ol' man afore y' screws 'im own' – 'You've come too far, en't ye? You've passed the

grave-yard' or 'It's a shame, I say, t' lose a loved one at a time like Christmas.'

After breakfast, we would help Dad decorate the front room. He obviously loved every minute of Christmas and went joyfully about the task of slinging paper-chains from the corners of the room to the electric light rose in the centre of the ceiling, sticking holly behind the pictures on the wall and entwining runners of ivy round the turned columns of the elaborate mahogany over-mantel. Coloured glass baubles, carefully saved from year to year, were hung amongst the greenery and a blue and silver blown-glass peacock with a long tail of silken plumage occupied the centre of the room clipped to a carpenter's pencil stuck into the side of the light-fitting.

As he climbed each chair in turn reaching up to fasten a paper bell to the ceiling with a drawing pin or tuck another spray of yew behind the curtain rail, he would sing an appropriate snatch of song:

> The mistletoe hung in the castle hall,
> The holly branch hung on the old oak wall,
> The Baron's retainers were blithe and gay
> All keeping their Christmas holiday . . .

His mood was infectious and we joined in with both the decorating and the singing with enthusiasm. Practically everything seemed to be a cue for a song. A cold wintry day would prompt:

> Crying, Father, I pray, let me in,
> Oh, come down and open the door,
> Or the child that I hold at my bosom will die,
> As the wind blows across the wild moor.

A fine, sunny morning would invite:

The morn was fair the sky was clear, no breath came over the sea,
When Mary left her highland cot and wandered forth with me. . .

This festive mood seemed to winkle out little fragments of song we seldom heard at other times and which never found their way into his song book becuse he didn't know all the words. Songs like 'Seventeen Come Sunday' and 'The Lawyer Bold' and 'No John No', all of which had been old Steady Petit's songs. After singing as much as he knew, he would reminisce on the old singers, as if he was thinking aloud.

After a couple of verses of 'Lord Thomas' he would add, 'Ol' Stevie Barrow's song – shepherd along with my brother Johnny – audacious ol' fella – could jump a five-bar gate when 'e wuz seventy (so 'e said) – used t' wear a mole-skin cap.' Or after a fragment of Dick Turpin he would say, 'Ah, that wuz ol' Fred Tearle – dirty ol' sod – used t' live down Golden Square.' 'I Wandered by the Brookside' had been Will Wales' song, 'A kind-hearted ol' chap – a straw trusser and flail thresher.' 'My ol' daddy used t' sing "The Bailiff's Daughter of Islington", but I don't think even he knew all the words.'

By twelve o'clock on Christmas morning the front room was bedecked and burgeoning like a green forest glade. The sideboard was laden with bottles of port wine and sherry, bowls of tangerines and nuts and boxes of dried figs, dates and crystallized fruits, while a fire crackled merrily in the hearth. Mother and two or three odd aunties were busy in the scullery cooking vegetables and preparing sauces and all the attendant etceteras without which the main ingredient – gently browning in Mr Hilder's oven – would not be fully appreciated, and steam from the Christmas pudding, as it bubbled gently in a large iron saucepan at the back of the hob, filled every nook and corner of the cottage with spicy, ambrosial aroma.

'Turkey-burds' ready for Christmas sale at Joye's shop, Pound Street, Petworth, 1930

The company, mostly relatives, was beginning to assemble with everyone in a jovial mood and on their best behaviour, showing off the ties, socks, handkerchiefs, and pairs of gloves they had received as presents that morning and as the glasses of wine were handed round, a vibrant sense of warmth and good fellowship prevailed. There was an air of excitement and the women-folk were becoming intensely concerned with laying the three tables, one in the front room, one in the kitchen and another in the scullery (for the children) which were necessary to get everyone seated. They scuttled in and out with plates, glasses, cutlery, and cruets, arranging and re-arranging fussily until the spread met their critical approval. The men, in an expansive mood, talked of Christmases gone by with the seats of their trousers to the fire and handling their unaccustomed cigars like cows with muskets, while we, the small fry, were left pretty much to our own devices.

One year our devices included surreptitiously filling our glasses with sherry instead of ginger wine and the holiday spirit suddenly slipped into top gear. Life put on a great big smile and Ron and I laughed and skylarked all the way down to the bakehouse to fetch the turkey and joint of beef. On the journey home with our succulent load swinging between us I had an inspiration. There had been a pretty sharp frost that morning and the pond was frozen over. One or two small children had been tentatively testing the strength of the ice but the chances of it bearing any substantial weight were slim. 'Ron,' I said, all valiant with sherry, 'we've never took the ol' bird across the pond before. Let's give 'er a try, shall us?' Ron mumbled dissenting noises behind me but as I was in the leading shafts he had no option but to follow me.

Gingerly easing one shiny, brown shoe in front of the other I edged forward on to the yielding ice. Ron kept up a rumble of protest at the back but I pushed on over the undulating surface. 'The more she bends the more she bears,' I cried. I was feeling buoyantly confident and we were already more than halfway across. 'Come on, we're goin' to make 'istory t'day, ol' kiddy,' I said. 'Yeah,' was the sardonic reply, 'we'll make 'istory all right, if we drop the bloody lot in the pond.'

Just then there was a fusillade of sound like rifle fire and I dropped through the ice and stood knee-deep in freezing water. The stretcher tilted dangerously and the two dishes started to slide forward and were only saved from a watery grave by Ron slowly sinking down behind me till he stood in the mud on the same level as I, restoring the stretcher to an even keel. It was a fearful moment. We took stock and, ignoring the state of our clothes, were thankful enough that the dinner was still intact.

With the crisis over, we sloshed ashore and on to the bank

where, with handfuls of grass, we wiped off the worst of the creamy, grey mud with which our best shoes and the trouser legs of our Sunday suits were plastered. 'I told y' it wouldn't bear,' said Ron as we squelched up the road leaving a sad, dripping trail behind us.

Back in the cottage the state of our clothes passed unnoticed in the excitement and bustle of dishing up what was generally considered to be the meal of the year. It was an unqualified success and, as we looked round at the happy faces munching away ecstatically at the loaded plates before them, we observed a diplomatic silence about how narrowly their dinner had avoided finishing up at the bottom of the duck-pond. Ron gave me a knowing wink and we tucked another guilty secret under our belts. . . .

Snow Harvest

ANDREW YOUNG

A white Christmas has become a rare event in Sussex in recent years but children still dream of waking to a new-made, snow-minted playground where all is magically white – a world of snowballs, tobogganing and fun.

The moon that now and then last night
Glanced between clouds in flight
Saw the white harvest that spread over
The stubble fields and even roots and clover.

One of George Garland's atmospheric snow scenes, actually taken in February 1940

It climbed the hedges, overflowed
And trespassed on the road,
Weighed down fruit-trees and when winds woke
From white-thatched roofs rose in a silver smoke.

How busy is the world today!
Sun reaps, rills bear away
The lovely harvest of the snow
While bushes weep loud tears to see it go.

Gooche's Strong Beer

JOHN HOLLAMBY

Varied as beverages now are, there is nothing like a Sussex ale at Christmas. Sadly, Sussex brewers are fewer now, but this song was composed in praise of the beer made by Thomas Gooche of Hailsham and published in 1827. A version of it was sung by the Patching shepherd, Michael Blann, who died in 1934, aged ninety, and is among the songs he wrote down in his song book (now in Worthing Museum).

'Fancy it Burgundy, only fancy it, and 'tis worth ten shillings a quart.'

Michael Blann, the Patching shepherd, then in his late eighties, pipes a tune. The picture was taken by Barclay Wills shortly before Blann's death

O, Gooche's beer your heart will cheer,
And put you in condition:
The man that will but drink his fill,
Has need of no physician.

'Twill fill your veins, and warm your brains,
And drive out melancholy;
Your nerves 'twill brace, and paint your face,
And make you fat and jolly.

The foreigners they praise their wines
('Tis only to deceive us):
Would they come here and taste this beer,
I'm sure they'd never leave us.

The meagre French their thirst would quench,
And find much good 'twould do them;
Keep them a year on Gooche's beer,
Their county would not know them.

All you that have not tasted it,
I'd have you set about it;
No man with pence and common sense
Would ever be without it.

Christmas Fare

LILIAN CANDLIN

In the early years of this century Christmas tea was a great occasion. Today the family is often so full up with the Christmas dinner, which in many homes is still served at mid-day, that they have no room for Christmas tea.

Teatime on Christmas day in Edwardian times was generally around five o'clock, when the family had had time to go for a walk to let their dinner settle down.

And my, what a spread it was! Sandwiches and cakes of all kinds, with the great centre piece of the Christmas cake, or biscuit as it was always called by my grandmother, in spite of her grandchildren repeatedly telling her that it was a cake, not a biscuit. She would reply with a chuckle 'My mother called it a biscuit and if biscuit was good enough for her it is good enough for me.'

Later, however, I discovered that as a Sussex woman she was correct. Parish, in his *Dictionary of Sussex Dialect* (1875) writes: 'In Sussex the words biscuit and cake interchange their usual meaning.' The writer of the *Cook's Oracle* (1822) also refers to this in a recipe for Christmas cake. She writes, 'The goodness of the cake or biscuit depends on it being well baked.'

She claimed that the secret for the goodness of her cake was due to the dripping which had come from the joint of beef that had been eaten on Stir-up Sunday. This is the last Sunday of the church's year, when the Collect repeated at Matins begins with the words 'Stir up we beseech Thee, O Lord.' The words of which are said to have been taken by the women in the congregation as a signal that it was time to start preparing for the great Christmas feast. It was really a feast in those days. Someone recently, when looking back on Christmas past said that the modern child has Christmas every day. She was right when you think of Edwardian days!

Much of the fare now connected with Christmas but eaten all the year round did not appear until Christmas in those days. Take oranges for instance. Up to the 1920s oranges were only in season from early December until early April. The only place in the days before refrigeration that sent oranges to England was Spain. At Christmas these were very sour. So much so that we were allowed to poke a hole in the skins and into the hole push a lump of sugar. The juice was then sucked through the sugar. At that time there was no bottled or tinned orange juice, so oranges were definitely a large part of Christmas, and every child hoped to see an orange sticking out of the top of their stocking.

Another fruit enjoyed at Christmas but hardly ever seen today was the medlar. This looks like a large brown rose hip. In fact, the medlar tree (*Mespilus germanica*) belongs to the rose family. The fruit is picked in late autumn, but they are not ready for eating until about Christmas, when they will have softened and the insides look like a rotten apple, with three large pips in the centre. Why this fruit has lost favour is surprising. To my mind medlars are delicious and are far superior to the exotic fruits that we are now persuaded to buy. Medlars could be bought in Brighton as late as the 1950s. As a school girl I bought many a half pint for twopence (old money). The greengrocer would measure them into a tall wooden measure, shaped rather like a jug. When he was in a good mood he would top the measure generously. Why people with large gardens don't plant medlar trees is a mystery. They are hardy and look lovely in the early summer when covered with blossom. There is a flourishing tree in the garden of Southover Grange, at Lewes, and another in the village of West Dean in East Sussex, on which I look with covetousness.

Perhaps the most important thing, however, was the Christmas cake. These in the shops today often appear to be of one style, but in the day of the one-man bakery shop, each one tried to outdo the shop along the road. So much so, that on the Sunday before Christmas the window blinds were left up and the cakes put on show for all to see. On the way to Sunday School in Brighton, two such shops had to be passed. One belonged to Mr Day and the other to Mr Parish. To these windows we glued our noses and often got late for school.

Both men used completely different designs. Mr Day, who had a shop in Upper St James Street, decorated his cakes in a

Children enjoying a Christmas shop window, 1956

most exciting way. How he did his decorations I have no idea. On top of each cake was a plain sheet of white icing, which had pictures on it that looked as though it had been drawn with a red crayon. There were skating scenes with ladies gliding across the ice with their hands tucked into muffs; children playing at snow-balling; Father Christmas on his sleigh and many others. Mr Parish iced his cakes in the more conventional manner, but here again the designs were many and varied.

A baker to whom I was talking about this icing of cakes said that the time that would have to be spent on icing original designs would today make the cakes far too costly. Alas! We all have more time than our forefathers but, when it comes to spending it at work, it just cannot be done. What a lot the children of today are missing!

A Vicarage Christmas

NOEL STREATFIELD

Noel Streatfield, author of Ballet Shoes, *has long been a favourite with children, but the story of her own Sussex upbringing during the Edwardian years is rather less widely known. Noel's father was a Church of England*

vicar – later, Bishop of Lewes – and Noel and her brother and two sisters grew up in a series of vicarages in the county. Noel was the second of the three girls: imaginative, rebellious, self-willed and less pretty than her sisters. In her childhood memoir, A Vicarage Family, *she appears as 'Victoria'.*

It was not like the Christmas at St Leonard's-on-Sea when, for days beforehand, the bell never stopped ringing as gifts of all kinds were delivered – but especially useful, helpful presents from the parishioners. In those days the tradespeople with whom you dealt sent presents: a turkey from the butcher; a box of crystallised fruits or chocolates from the grocer; fruit from the greengrocer. Even the local undertaker sent a present of wine. Tradespeople's presents still turned up, but at Eastbourne there were fewer presents from the parishioners, though the children's father received enough and from such unexpected sources to make him feel quite overcome.

'How kind they are, dear people,' he said as he received for his wife yet another pot plant or, for the children, chocolates or something for himself. 'I really expected nothing, my first Christmas here.'

Then off the children's father would dash, his arms full of little books on Christian subjects which he had signed for his friends, for it was a strict rule in the family that for a present received one was sent. Even when they were tiny the children were taught this and would work laboriously at home-made gifts. Granny, who even when the children were small was not much good at getting about, still cherished a book-marker made by Victoria just before her sixth birthday. Its text, in cross stitch, said *Hop on hop ever*. Even now, though they had less time, the girls made many Christmas presents, some of which were put away as emergency gifts to send to the unexpected giver: simple presents such as lavender bags; emery cushions for rusty needles; pen-wipers and needle- books; but, no doubt being home-made, they pleased.

There were some things that were new about the Eastbourne Christmas. Always the family had been used to carol singers who came into the hall to sing and afterwards were given ginger wine and mince pies. But this year, as well as carol singers, hand-bell ringers arrived. They stood in a circle pealing out the old favourites while the family sat on the stairs to listen.

'There is something about bells,' Isobel said after the bell-ringers had gone. 'As they rang I sort of felt Christmas come into the house.'

Another feature of that Christmas was the curate. Curates came and curates went and, except on special occasions, the children seldom saw them to talk to because their father kept his curates' noses to the grindstone. But the curates usually came to Christmas lunch and, unless they had anywhere better to go, stayed on for tea and the Christmas tree – and dull and shy the children found them.

That year the curate – a man called Plimsol, known to the children as Mr Cassock because he seldom seemed to wear anything else – came to lunch. Right away he set a new standard for curates by arriving with five boxes of Fuller's chocolates. A box of chocolates of their own was highly thought of by the children, for most of the boxes received were family boxes and were stored in a cupboard to be passed round before bed, when each child was allowed one. So individual boxes from which the children were allowed, with permission, to help themselves were much valued. But that was not all; when the crackers were pulled Mr Plimsol found a blue sun-bonnet in his and not only put it on but sang:

'Oh, what have you got for dinner, Mrs Bond?' in a delightfully silly way.

'Bags I you for my team for charades this evening,' said John.

A folded card which opens to offer Christmas greetings. The photograph shows a young woman, possibly the sender, dressed up in a pantomime costume

Always for Christmas tea and the tree afterwards the vicarage doors were thrown open to those who were lonely or had nowhere else to go. Annie, on hearing the Christmas arrangements, made a remark which became a family quotation: 'As at Sandringham.'

Either because of the success of Mr Plimsol in the charades or because some special quality surrounded that Christmas, it stayed in the children's memory.

Their mother always decorated the tree and they were never allowed to see it until the candles were lit. That year the tree stood in the small annexe to the drawing-room – a perfect place because there were curtains which could be drawn back when the tree was to be seen in all its glory. That year there were about fifteen waifs and strays, mostly women, all rather

Petworth School treat in Christmas 1939, giving pleasure to the children in the shadow of war

shy and sad while they drank tea and ate Victoria's birthday – now the Christmas – cake.

When the tea was cleared, Annie and Hester joined the party, and soon everyone was circling the tree singing 'The First Nowell' and then 'Good King Wenceslas', with John singing the King's verses and Victoria the page's. Then came the time to strip the tree. The majority of the parcels were for the family of course, but no one was allowed to feel left out, so there were plenty of little gifts for the guests. Annie and Hester (Miss Herbert went to a brother for Christmas) had presents from every member of the family and, as well as proper presents from the children's parents, each received an afternoon apron. Annie said when she opened her parcel:

'Thank you, madam. It will save you buying me one for when you want me to bring in tea on Hester's day out.'

The present-giving over and the wrappings swept up, the charades started and, as had been hoped, Mr Plimsol proved a natural comic. It was lovely to see the lonely rather sad people who had arrived, mopping the tears of laughter off their cheeks.

Then were was more carol singing and then the guests were in the hall putting on their wraps, and another Christmas Day was over.

Usually Boxing Day was thank-you-letter day, with a little rehearsing for the Boxing even show, but that Boxing Day there could be no letter writing for everyone had taken John's advice for, though there were no elves, there was scarcely a moment when a chorus of sorts was not entering, so that as many children as possible might be used.

There was a simple story running through the play of a bewitched princess lost in a wood who was rescued by a gallant prince. But to the audience the high sports were when their offspring appeared as toad-stools, clouds, flowers or fairies, all of which lived in the wood.

The talent was probably nil and Victoria's ability to arrange dances was non-existent, but it was all very cheerful and fast-moving, and Louise was excellent thumping away on the piano. But there were two high spots: Isobel's dresses and John's lighting. Isobel had let herself go, and many of the clothes she had designed were really charming. Few had any money for luxuries, but there was butter-muslin and there was dye. So her clouds danced in grey frocks with rose pink petticoats and rose pink stockings, and her flowers, however awkwardly they moved, almost looked like the real thing.

To add to Isobel's dresses John, with Dick as assistant, with lamps and coloured papers produced what was generally considered stupendous effects. Certainly the audience were more than pleased. 'Proper professional,' they said. 'Better than the panto at the theatre, shouldn't wonder.'

Victoria took a curtain as author, Louise as pianist, the boys for their lighting and Isobel for her designs and they were all cheered. But the best moment was talking it over afterwards over cups of cocoa. The children's father said:

'Bless you all, that play will work wonders, it was just what the parish needed.'

Boxing Day Letter, 1913

ELEANOR FARJEON

The poet Edward Thomas, whose adopted home was the Hampshire village of Steep, close to the county border, was a frequent visitor to Sussex. He was often at the Meynells' estate at Greatham and stayed for long periods at the home of Vivian Locke Ellis, Selsfield House, East Grinstead. It was while he and his family were spending Christmas at Selsfield that he wrote in thanks to Eleanor Farjeon, whom he and his wife, Helen, had befriended. The date, 1913, gives an added poignancy to the passage. It was to be the last Christmas of peace before the outbreak of the war which was to rob Helen of her beloved Edward and England of one of her finest poets. The extract comes from Eleanor's moving tribute to Edward and Helen, Edward Thomas: The Last Four Years.

While Edward was staying indefinitely in East Grinstead, coming less often to town, I continued to go down to Steep to stay with Helen. It was during these days, and especially in the nights when we talked late, that the love between us came into full being.

'My wife could be the happiest woman on earth, if I would let her.' The truth is, Helen was oftener and more fully happy

than any wife I knew. Her happiness was an inexhaustible well; its zest enhanced the good days, and was her source of power against the dark ones. If Edward knew that Hamlet was written for him, he knew too that Helen was no Ophelia, and whatever he was and did she would not drown.

The greatest gift which he and she gave me in common was in being their unreserved selves while I was with them, sharing with me both what was painful and what was happy in their lives. The three children and I were completely friends. While Bronwen continued my education out-of-doors, Helen inside the house taught me some principles of cottage cooking, at which she was superb. She loved defeating poverty by providing ample dishes out of nothing, she rejoiced in her strong health that could carry all loads. Being and doing were almost one thing to her. Now when I came for a night or a week-end the pattern was changed. There were still the rambles, the impulsive picnics because the day was too good to be wasted, the shared work of the house, the long sitting in talk over the good meals. I missed, and she how much more, the serene hour when Edward, pipe in mouth, knelt on the hearthrug by Baba in her warm bath, humming, it seemed, through the very stem of the clay, Welsh tunes with their native words, while he soaped the baby's chubby body and towelled it on his knee. We missed the after-supper hour when he read to us. Now, supper over, when the kitchen was 'redded up', instead of going to bed Helen made tea. She was avid for the friends she loved and could pour out her heart to, and we became midnight gossips, stirring our cups over the fire, and talking of people, of books, of our families, of our lives, of Edward. At one or two o'clock I might make a move—

'Oh *no*, Eleanor! not *yet*! I see you so *seldom*.'

More tea was made, we talked on till three or four.

One night when we had been talking only of Edward, of their first meeting, their early marriage, and his dark diffi-

Another Victorian cut-out card: the face of an angel shining from the cresent moon

culties, I said, 'You know what I feel for him, don't you; you know I love him?'

'Yes, Eleanor, I do.'

'If it hurts you or him, if it ever could, I can go out of your lives now, rather than cause any pain.'

'Oh my darling! you mustn't *ever* go.' She put her arms round me and said, 'If having you could make him any happier, I'd give him to you gladly.'

These words, said in utmost truth from one woman to another, I find hard even now to write down, but without them our story would be incomplete.

Christmas drew near. Helen prepared to join Edward at Selsfield House with the children. I went back to Fellows Road

and our rich and multitudinous Christmas plans; and for the first time packed a huge and varied parcel for the five Thomases, crammed with nice presents and nonsense ones gaily-wrapped, and labelled against being opened till Christmas morning.

On Boxing Day Edward wrote me his last letter of the year.

at Selsfield House.

My dear Eleanor

Little did I think as I carried that parcel up from the station that it contained an electric flashlight for me. Sometimes I believe that you sent it just because it would be useful, sometimes that it is an earthly object with a heavenly meaning, sometimes that its purpose was to see what I should say about it. So that naturally it is hard to know which of the three possible letters I ought to write; harder still to write them all; quite easy not to write any one of them, I mean after Christmas day. But you should have seen that parcel opened. The surprise of the five people concerned was as great as when all the animals in Eden had names given them, & the pleasure as great as that of the couples who were chosen for the Ark. Mine being the most practised, indefatigable, undryable pen, I suppose it ought to set about painting the picture which the Farjeons painted with the flesh of five Thomases upon the canvas of Christmas Day. But the fact is that I mulled the claret yesterday.

Goodbye. I hope I shall be able to arrange to come to Cliffords before long & see you there, having recovered from the drinking of claret which I mulled yesterday. I hope it will not constantly reappear in my pen like this, in fact that I shall get it completely out of my system & tell you what a

lot of cheerfulness we got out of everything else & especially that finely selected and masterfully packed box from Fellows Road. If only you could have included some of yourselves in the box! For excellent as the elements are – Ellises, Coxes & Thomases – still, somehow, I don't know. However.

Yours ever,
Edward Thomas.

The Boxgrove Tipteers

HARDIMAN SCOTT

The survival of Sussex folk tradition depends upon the quiet determination of those who refuse (very much against the grain of our times) to allow them to die. In this chapter from Secret Sussex, *Hardiman Scott paid tribute to R.J. Sharp, who did so much to keep alive the old Sussex tradition of Christmas Mumming, or 'Tipteering', as we call it, after the local 'tippet', a cloak or disguise.*

In a room packed with books, manuscripts, old-bound versions of folk-songs, files, papers, oddments and curios and old sheep bells and cow bells, each recalling life as it used to be

lived and played in a rural Sussex of the past, John and I found Mr R.J. Sharp still striving to keep alive some of the ancient traditions of his county, and, moreover, keeping them alive in a natural way.

Mr Sharp has revived the centuries-old Christmas mummers' play among a group of Sussex villagers and has helped to restore the folk-song and dance to their integral place in local culture. Nevertheless, in this room of his Chichester home, redolent with so much tradition, he was rather pessimistic as to how long the revival could be maintained. Sturdy and genial, with a conversational style that ambles and rambles over his interest in Sussex folk-lore and legend, and darts hither and thither on little quests of speculation, Mr Sharp lamented the fall of the large country estates, for they were, he maintained, an essential setting for the mummers' play. But I felt that this was a small problem against Mr Sharp's own enthusiasm and his belief in the importance of the folk-song, dance and play in our traditional life. There proved to be a more practical difficulty. Throughout the war he, together with members of the Boxgrove Tipteers, as the Sussex mummers are called, had little sessions at his own house regularly every week or fortnight to sing the old Sussex folk-songs. All the time he has played his fiddle for the singers. But now, the war over and the Boxgrove Tipteers planning to produce their play again, the fiddler has developed arthritis in his fingers. This irony of circumstance is unfortunate to say the least, and one which Mr Sharp naturally feels keenly. But the folk-singing will somehow go on, and he is hopeful that some younger members of the Tipteers will come forward to carry on the tradition which he has maintained for so many years.

The Christmas mummers' play, of course, was once a normal feature of seasonal festivities. The players used to sing their way across the countryside, blowing their cows' horns to

announce their arrival, and then entertain in the large country houses. Now the tradition lingers in only a few places, and the Boxgrove Tipteers, I think I am right in saying, are the only mummers still performing in Sussex, although other 'gangs' have formerly existed at Angmering, Midhurst, Hove, West Stoke, East Preston, Iping, Washington, Petworth, Horsham, East Dean, East Marden, West Wittering, Westbourne, Compton and Ferring.

Mr Sharp's story goes back to 1912, when he was living at East Preston. At Christmas of that year the local Tipteers went to his house and performed their play. From this initial interest the real revival began.

'I discovered the play had only been revived the previous year,' he told us, 'by a Mr Foard, who had lived and worked as a farm labourer in the village all his life. He remembered as a boy going out tipteering with an old man named Barnard, and Barnard apparently took the money they received and rewarded his young helpers with sweets. Foard had written out the play entirely from memory and from the recollections of some old people who had formerly seen it. His version was pretty accurate, although it was clearly incomplete in places.'

From Mr Frank Dawtrey, a cowman of Norman descent, who lived at Iping and who had also remembered several old Sussex folk-songs and the only two recorded Sussex dances for men, 'The Bonny Breast Knot' and 'Over the Sticks', Mr Sharp was able to obtain the Iping version of this play, which is sometimes called *St George and the Turkish Knight*. By a careful combination of both versions, the present play was evolved, and at Christmas, 1913, was played in all the large country houses of the East Preston district.

By 1927, when Mr Sharp went to live at Chichester, he had, of course, become more engrossed in folk-dancing, and soon discovered the Boxgrove Folk-Dancing Club. He played the fiddle for the dances, and suggested that they should revive the

tipteers. From then on and until the outbreak of war the Boxgrove Tipteers presented their mummers' play every Christmas.

But this was not all. As Mr Sharp unfolded his story we heard him use one of his favourite phrases. 'We decided,' he said, 'between the tipteering, to turn ourselves into a "living museum of Sussex folk-songs".'

In the 'Anglesea Arms' at Halnaker, the Tipteers met regularly and learnt the old Sussex songs.

'Each man,' said Mr Sharp, 'had a book in which he wrote the words as I read them out. Then I used to play the tune three or four times on my fiddle, and very soon the men had both the notes and the words perfect.'

Indeed, the tipteers became as unique for their songs as for their play, and in 1913 and 1937 took part in the National Festival of English Folk-Song and Dance at the Albert Hall. At both festivals they sang 'The Moon shone Bright', a beautiful carol which only the Tipteers possess and which is included in the mummers' play. Although they were once televised, the tipteers have never been broadcast or recorded.

'It would be absolutely impossible,' said Mr Sharp. 'A broadcast or a recording would destroy all the intimacy and atmosphere that is so much a part of both the songs and the play. They are something which just cannot be convincingly translated into a modern medium.'

The play itself is a most curious and interesting piece of drama. It lasts for about twenty minutes, and, in Mr Sharp's words, 'is a quaint jumble of religion and clownishness'. It has for its characters Father Christmas, Noble Captain, St. George (or sometimes King George) Prince of Peace, Turkish Knight, Valiant Soldier, Doctor, Little Jolly Jack, and the Fiddler.

Father Christmas introduces himself to the house with the words: 'In come I, old Father Christmas, be I welcome, or be I b'aint?' And he pauses for the master of the house to reply.

The story tells of the Noble Captain, 'just lately come from France', who boasts what he would do with St George if he were there. St George obligingly comes in, there is an argument and a sword fight. They are parted by the Prince of Peace, who makes his only appearance with the words:

'In come I, the Prince of Peace,
For at this time all blood and warfare now must cease.'

After the players sing 'The Sussex Mummers' Carol', the Turkish Knight enters, and he fights with St. George's man, the Valiant Soldier. The Knight is killed, and the Doctor arrives to perform a miracle that raises the Turk from death, after an altercation with Father Christmas about the cost of his professional services.

Little Jolly Jack does not make his appearance until the end of the play, and seems more an excuse to ask the household (or audience) to show their appreciation of the play in kind. He says:

'In come I, Little Jolly Jack,
My wife and family all upon my back.
Though my family be but small,
I can scarce find bread and cheese for them all.
Christmas comes but once a year
And when it comes it brings good cheer.
Roast beef, plum pudding and mince pie,
Who likes these any better than I
Christmas fare makes us dance and sing.
Money in the purse is a capital thing.
Ladies and gentlemen give what you please,
Old Father Christmas will welcomely receive.'

There follows the dance, 'Over the Sticks', which was

Cover picture of the first and only issue of *The Sussex Garland*, a brave attempt by editor Pam Allsop to provide a new and much needed magazine in the great tradition of Arthur Beckett's inspired *Sussex County Magazine* (1926–1956)

introduced in order to preserve it and which is danced by four men over crossed stocks, and the play ends with a nonsense dialogue and a carol.

In origin, it would seem to be pagan, deriving from the rites performed by primitive men to encourage the sun to awaken the winter earth into growth again, and there are phrases like, 'which strikes a light in his whole body'. But it has both absorbed and been modified by Christian influences. The ritual of beseeching the earth to live again has been transformed into the miracle of raising a man from the dead, or almost the dead, for his limbs are broken and Father Christmas has already been speculating on the size of coffin needed. When the miracle is performed by the character enigmatically called 'Doctor', he assures the audience: 'As you see, ladies and gentlemen, I am no quack doctor, running about the State telling a pack of lies; I'm a real Spanish doctor, and can cure the sick and raise the dead before your eyes.' This probably dates to the time when southern Spain was the seat of learning under the Moors.

Mr Sharp has also an ingenious and, I think, likely theory that the miracle performed by the Doctor has some relation to the Ash Wednesday of 1218 when the abbess and nuns of St. Sextus heard news that the Lord Napoleon, nephew of Cardinal Stephen who was present, had been thrown from his horse and killed. St Dominic prayed over the body, rose, and making the sign of the Cross, commanded Napoleon to arise 'in the name of Our Lord Jesus Christ', whereupon it is said that the Lord Napoleon returned to life. Mr Sharp points out that the doctor, in saying 'Saddle my horse, Jack, I'll be gone', is the only character who refers to a horse although St George and the Noble Captain are persons who would use horses, and also that, although the dead man has been struck down by a thrust of the sword, he is referred to as having 'Legs broke, arms broke, finnicking gout in his great toe'. The Doctor produces a box of pills and a bottle of Golden Philosopher Drops, puts one in the dead man's mouth, and a drop from the bottle on his nose and on his temple. In doing this, incidentally, he almost makes the sign of the Cross.

The Crusades have also had their effect on the play, and there is doubtless an infiltration of Elizabethan influences: in fact, some of the dialogue is suggestive of political inferences in that time.

Towards the end, there is a curious dialogue beginning, 'Hip, Mr Carpenter', a phrase uttered by the doctor to the Noble Captain, and followed by the doctor adding: 'I've got a little question to ask you. How far is it across the river?' The whole cast then chants:

> 'When you're in the middle, you're half way over,
> When you're in the middle, you're half way over.
> Fol de riddle ido – Fol de riddle ido.'

The thing progresses with a series of riddles, each beginning with a 'Hip, Mr Carpenter', and ending with a 'Fol de riddle ido'. This, I understand, is derived from a French shadow pantomime, *Ombres chinoises*, which became popular in this country towards the end of the eighteenth century.

For the play, the players wear appropriate costumes, but when giving a performance of folk-songs only, they dress in smocks (or round-frocks), some of them being family heirlooms that have been handed down for generations. Others are copies made by the Ticehurst Women's Institute, which keeps the art of smocking alive.

And in the tipteering atmosphere of Mr Sharp's study, we naturally felt eager to see a performance of *St George and the Turkish Knight*. When? Mr Sharp turned over the pages of the play that he knows so well, took down his old fiddle, and said reflectively, as he tried his fingers on the strings: 'Ah, I don't know. I'd like to think it was soon. It will be a tragedy if it dies out. We're carrying on with the folk-songs, and I hope one or two of the younger ones will keep the Tipteers alive, although it is likely to be some time before we can present another performance.'

Secretly I felt sure that, after the years of work, Mr Sharp would not let this tradition die without a struggle or be satisfied with his 'living museum of folk-songs' alone. The men about him are of fine Sussex stock – carpenters, labourers, woodmen and gardeners, men who are likely to want to preserve their play out of an instinctive desire to maintain a tradition that is part of their lives.

Christmas Hauntings

R. THURSTON HOPKINS

Thurston Hopkins – literary pilgrim, windmill enthusiast, founder of the Society of Sussex Downsmen – was a remorseless seeker of things 'Sussex'. Here he recalls his encounter with a local ghost, with which, it seems, Sussex is well stocked.

Sussex ghosts? Nearly every historical building and landmark in our country boasts a ghost. There are a round dozen of them

at Brighton, not counting the notorious phantom lady, dressed in white and possessing long yellow hair, who hovers around White Hawk Camp.

The Manor of Leechpool, which nestles under Cissbury Ring, has a ghost, which is only what might be expected of a solitary spot bearing a name indicating a pool overstocked with leeches, but I am rather of the opinion that it is the debased rendering of lich-pole, meaning a gallows-tree.

The ghost of Leechpool Manor is a highwayman who was hanged by the side of the old downland coach-road, running between Lancing and Steyning.

When he walked to the gallows he vowed that he would never sleep in his grave, which had been dug in the centre of the road, so that all the coaches would rattle and bump over his bones.

Of all speculative theories, that of Dr John Dee, the sixteenth-century alchemist, sends the most thrills up one's spine. He said that none of the dead ever come back, but some of them refuse to leave. The highwayman of Leechpool was one of the kind who overstayed his welcome. He was lowered into his grave and the earth piled on top, but on the next morning his body had lifted the soil away and his head had sprung up like a dreadful jack-in-the-box. Several times was the body replaced, with the same result. Tradition does not disclose how many times the highwayman popped up before he settled in his grave. However, his ghostly counterpart, mounted on a ghostly horse ever afterwards haunted this Downland trackway.

An old Downland farmer named Parkyn, in whose family the tradition of the phantom highwayman has lingered for a hundred years or so, told me that a driver of a coach near the spot was held up by what he imagined to be a real highwayman, and, making up his mind to 'run the fellow down,' he whipped up his horses to a furious gallop, with the result that horses and coach passed *clean through* the intruder.

Christmas card of two black cats dancing, *c.* 1890–1900

Sinister tales were told by farm labourers who passed over the haunted road at nightfall; they declared that their wagons bumped over *something* stretched athwart the road, and when they looked for the obstruction there was nothing to be seen at all.

On the west side of Hurstmonceaux Castle is a room called 'the Drummer's Hall.' It is traditionally reputed to be haunted

by the spirit of a giant drummer that was always heard drumming before a death in the Fiennes family. One member of the family, young Thomas Fiennes, Lord Dacre of Hurstmonceaux, seeking some new thrill in a life already given over to reckless gaiety, resolved to hunt by moonlight. All would have been well had Dacre hunted over his own land. He, however, hunted Sir Nicholas Pelham's deer and fell foul of the knight's keepers. A fray ensued and Lord Dacre wielded a wicked sword. One of the keepers afterwards died from his wounds and Dacre was arrested for murder. Three other young huntsmen who had taken part in the affray were charged with Dacre.

Since the gamekeeper met his death in a brawl, it was generally supposed that Dacre and his three companions would escape the gallows. After all, the fatal blow was struck without malice or premeditation.

The Drummer of Hurstmonceaux, however, sensed death in the air, and his phantom drum throbbed through the night.

Then there are the ghosts at Bramber Castle. I can speak about them from first-hand information. Some years ago I finished a twenty-mile walk across the Downs at Bramber, and, considering that I was fully entitled to quench my thirst with a cool flagon of ale, I called in to see my friend, Mr Weekes, at the 'King's Head,' Beeding. I finished my tankard of ale – well, h'm, yes; it might have been two or three tankards – and retired to a comfortable grass-bank at Bramber Castle to rest. I must have slumbered for an hour or so. Suddenly I was awakened by a cry that turned the darkness livid, and some horrible white thing was hovering over my face. Surely this is the ghost of Maud of Ditchling, who holds the haunting rights of the castle, was my first thought. Ah! how mistaken one can be about ghosts! My ghost was a large white owl which had flopped down on me and had screeched with anger at finding an intruder on his property.

The real ghost of Bramber Castle is De Lindfield, the lover of Maud of Ditchling. Maud was the wife of Hubert de Hurst, but she carried on an illicit love affair with De Lindfield. Lord Hubert discovered his wife's indiscreet love-making, whereupon he ordered De Lindfield to be immured in the tower (portions of which still stand near the church), and, after building a wall in front of the doorway of his prison, left him to die. Maud died a raving lunatic through hearing the dreadful moans of her lover.

Now the spirits of the demented lovers are supposed to haunt the castle – but I am told that the pair of them, either as ghosts or real-life characters, are historically quite inadmissible.

Keeper's Revenge

Boxing Day field sports are traditional in Sussex, as elsewhere, and, as often as not, a meet of the hunt, or a pheasant shoot, will provide some incident which becomes, in the retelling, a story to be enjoyed in the tap-room of some out-of-the-way village pub years after. My own favourite concerns the Boxing Day shoot on a certain estate where the shooting is let to a syndicate. I relate it much as it was told to me.

'Now, as I expect you know, the Keeper, as is usually the case, gets certain gifts, called perquisites, besides his cottage and

The Leconfield Meet on Boxing Day 1934 at the Gog and Magog, Petworth Park

his wages. Among these is the tradition that whoever downs a white pheasant – of which but a handful are bred among thousands – should pay Keeper a fiver. A few years back, a new gun – a London chap, I think he was – brings a white one down and Keeper, as is his right, puts out his hand for his money. To his surprise, this chap refuses to pay, causing, as you can imagine, great offence.

'Well, when Keeper gets home his wife can see at once that he's upset, but, having been told of the incident by one of the beaters, and being a wise woman, she keeps mum. Later, after he has warmed himself a glass or two of her excellent sloe gin, she sees a smile spread over his face and a certain look come into his eye. "Hm!" he says to her, "That'll teach him, reckon'" – but he never tells her what he means by this and she knows better than to ask.

'I'd heard about the little matter of the white pheasant, but having heard nothing more had forgotten until I was taking a stroll in the little valley under the beech hanger the following summer. It was a few days after the pheasants had been released from their pens. Now, as I was doddling along, I saw first one white bird, and then another, and then another. In all, I must have counted fifty of the white pheasants there in the valley . . . and then I remembered what his wife had told me about the look in the Keeper's eye!'

What is Winter?

EDMUND BLUNDEN

Edmund Blunden was not a Sussex poet, but he had many Sussex connections, and could fairly claim, 'I sing of the rivers and hamlets and woodlands of Sussex and Kent, Such as I know them. . .' He was educated at Christ's Hospital, fought in the Royal Sussex Regiment during the First World War, and had his first collection of verses printed, as Shelley had done, in Horsham. Although he later left England, the Weald remained a source of inspiration.

The haze upon the meadow
  Denies the dying year,
For the sun's within it, something bridal

Is more than dreaming here.
There is no end, no severance,
No moment of deliverance,
No quietus made,
Though quiet abounds and deliverance moves
In that sunny shade.

What is winter? a word,
A figure, a clever guess.
That time-word does not answer to
This drowsy wakefulness.
The secret stream scorns interval
Though the calendar shouts one from the wall;
The spirit has no last days;
And death is no more dead than this
Flower-haunted haze.

Winter in West Downland

W.H. HUDSON

The spectacle of winter sunrise over the Sussex hills – that slow, unfolding, umbilical redness of a Downland dawn – encourages many a rambler to get out into the open air early on Boxing-Day morning. Whether you are wanting

to walk off your Christmas dinner, or prefer to enjoy your natural history from the comfort of a fireside armchair, there is no finer book to inspire you to see that winter landscape afresh than W.H. Hudson's Nature in Downland.

Better days than those spent in roughest weather on the hills I could not well have known. 'Oh, but you should visit this part of downland in spring!' I was told again and again. It was good enough in mid-winter in spite of weather of the kind we call bad; so good indeed as to make me somewhat sceptical as to its far greater attractiveness in summer. Is there anything in rural England more gratifying to the eye than a winter prospect in this green diversified country, with leafless beechen woods spread over slopes and summits, and gathered like darkest purple clouds within the combes and hollows of the great round hills!

Glad as I was to be out in wind and rain and snow on the summits, it was often a relief to escape from so furious a blast by going down to the sheltered weald, the flat, wooded country between Midhurst and Harting, where I loved to walk, and where these rambles had to end. I walked by the Rother, that fairest Sussex river, among the brown and purple woods, and darker pine. Walking there one day about noon, when the sky was a very soft blue, with a few fleecy grey clouds floating in it, and the wind was still, I came to a wide heath somewhere between Midhurst and Trotton. It was very silent; only two sounds were audible, and I stood for some time listening to them. One was the sound of a boy singing. He was a cow-boy; I could see him out in the middle of the heath, standing among the furze-bushes, where his cows were grazing. He was perhaps a choir-boy in one of the village churches; at all events, he was singing a hymn in a trained and very beautiful voice. In that still, open air, at the distance I heard him (two to three hundred yards), the voice seemed purer and sweeter than any boy's voice I have ever heard in any church or cathedral. No doubt it was the distance, the silence of nature, the wild, solitary scene, and perhaps, too, the abundant moisture in the air, that gave the voice its exceeding beauty; and the effect was as if this sound, too, had been cleansed and clarified by the rains, even as the sky had been washed to that softest, lucid blue. I listened to the boy singing and singing, with a short interval after each verse, and to the one other sound, which came to me from an equal distance on the opposite side – the singing of a solitary missel-thrush. The clear, bell-like note of the bird filled the intervals in the boy's singing; and the bird, like the boy, had a clearer, purer voice on that day; and like the other, too, he sang verse after verse, with short intervals between. The effect was indescribably beautiful.

* * *

At Chilgrove there is a wood which, seen at a distance, looks almost as uniformly dark as the famous yew grove at Kingly Bottom; but although the yew abounds greatly in it and the trees are well grown, throwing out immense horizontal branches near the ground, giving it that dark and sombre aspect, it is on a nearer view found to be composed of all the trees and bushes characteristic of the chalk downs – yew, beech, holly, thorn, juniper, furze, and wild clematis. It grows on the side, near the top, of a long, steep, hanger-like hill, and overhangs the Chilgrove vale. A wilder and more beautiful wood of that peculiar type found only among the west Sussex Downs I had never seen. Most of it was an almost impenetrable thicket and tangle, and in the open spaces the foot sank deep in the thick growth of softest moss. Here were the largest furze and juniper bushes I have seen in Sussex, the

One of George Garland's classic snow scenes. Children with toboggan at West Burton, near Bury, West Sussex in January 1940

junipers being, some of them, poplar and cypress shaped, and others with wide-spreading branches, looking like yews of a lively green. Some were fifteen to eighteen feet high, with a girth of two to three feet; and some of the yew-shaped bushes had branches six to eight feet in length. Here I observed that the great masses of black-green yew-tree foliage formed a wonderfully effective background to the feathery foliage of the juniper, a bright but very delicate glaucous green.

On the edge of this wood I found that curiosity in plant life – a perfect wild clematis tree. As a rule when a thorn tree, robbed of light and air by a too luxuriant clematis spread over it, perishes and finally crumbles to dust, the semi-parasite dies after it, being unable to keep itself up, or to live when prostrate on the earth. Occasionally, however, it does succeed in keeping off the ground for a time, but in most cases it has a widowed, forlorn appearance, swayed about this way and that on its too slender stem, its head bowed down, and the long attenuated twigs drooping like loosened hair to the earth. Here is a clematis that has a different aspect, with a round, straight, and shapely trunk, twenty-seven inches in circumference; its height is eighteen feet, and its innumerable fine pendulous branches give it the appearance of a weeping-willow tree. At the end of January when I saw it, it was still clothed in down as with a silver-grey fluffy foliage.

On the north escarpment of the downs, at this point, there are some fine yew groves and woods in the deep combes and hollows and ravine-like clefts in the sides of the hills. The finest of these is on the north side of the great down west of West Dean woods. Here in the side of the hill, there is an immense basin-shaped combe, its sloping circular sides covered with a dense dark growth of yews, and under these, the flat bottom of the basin is filled with a beechen wood. Seated on the turf on the rim of this great hollow in the side of the hill, one evening in late January, I had beneath me a scene to make a man's heart glad. I had only just discovered this hidden wood, and it came as a complete surprise; nothing quite like it had I seen before. In summer, when the beeches would appear from above as a floor of deep uniform green, there would not perhaps have been any special beauty in this spot. Winter had given the charm and magical effect it had for me on that evening, when the sun was going down in a cold but very clear sky. For the tall beeches on which I looked down appeared as innumerable white or pale columns standing on a floor of red and russet gold, and white columns and golden floor were all the more beautiful for being seen through the almost cloud-like tracery of innumerable purple and purplish-red or 'murrey'-coloured branchlets. The rich colour of that temple and palace of nature – the gold floor and purple roof – made the wide band of the yew seem black by contrast; and above the black yews the smooth turf of the hill-top looked a pale green.

One thing that added greatly to the charm of this wood was the vast multitude of wood-pigeons which were congregated in it. It was, I found, their favourite roosting-place in this neighbourhood. Alarmed at my presence they began to rush out of the trees on all sides in numbers, the sudden sharp clatter of their wings sounding at a distance like castanets. By-and-by they were all on the wing, gathered in one immense flock, rushing about this way and that in the vast wooded hollow beneath my feet, looking at times almost white as they streamed over the black yews and caught the level sunbeams on their upper plumage. This flock could not have numbered less than two to three thousand birds. Finally they began to settle on the beeches; and when all had settled, and with my powerful binoculars I had brought them so close to me as to be able to see distinctly all the delicate shading of their plumage and the brighter colours of beak and eye, I had before me as fascinating a tree-and-bird scene as it is possible to imagine.

The colour and grace of it could not be described – the multitude of birds, thick as starlings in the purple branches, not yet recovered from their alarm, but every one still moving its head and flirting its tail, and evidently anxious to keep an eye on the suspicious-looking (although gunless) intruder on their privacy.

Of all man's inventions, this is to me the most like a divine gift – this double tube in my hand, which enables me to follow the beautiful children of the air in their flight; and when they are at home and safe in woods, and on green waves, and on cliffs, to sit or float as it were invisible and unsuspected among them.

West of the wooded spots I have described in the neighbourhood of West Dean, the charm of this part of the downland country if anything increases; until, at Up Park and South Harting, when we are on the border of Hampshire, and can no further go, we are in the midst of the most beautiful scenery of the West Sussex Downs.

To a Snowflake

FRANCIS THOMPSON

One of my favourite walks at Storrington takes me over the meadow beside White Canons Monastery, where Francis Thompson took refuge for a year while seeking an opium cure.

What heart could have thought you? –
  Past our devisal
(O filigree petal!)
Fashioned so purely,
Fragilely, surely,
From what Paradisal
Imagineless metal,
Too costly for cost?
Who hammered you, wrought you,
From argentine vapour? –
'God was my shaper.
Passing surmisal,
He hammered, He wrought me,
From curled silver vapour,
To lust of His mind: –
Thou couldst not have thought me!
So purely, so palely,
Tinily, surely,
Mightily, frailly,
Insculped and embossed
With His hammer of wind,
And His graver of frost.'

Pooh's Song

A.A. MILNE

Pooh Bear is very much a Sussex bear. He came here with Christopher Robin when his parents bought Cotchford Farm, near Hartfield, on the fringes of Ashdown Forest. It was in the meadows and woods nearby that Christopher Robin and Pooh chose to live and had such adventures. Here was Posingford Wood, where Christopher Robin met the charcoal burner; and Pooh-sticks Bridge.

One day when Pooh Bear had nothing else to do, he thought he would do something, so he went round to Piglet's house to see what Piglet was doing. It was still snowing as he stumped over the white forest track, and he expected to find Piglet warming his toes in front of his fire, but to his surprise he saw that the door was open, and the more he looked inside the more Piglet wasn't there.

'He's out,' said Pooh sadly. 'That's what it is. He's not in. I shall have to go on a fast Thinking Walk by myself. Bother!'

But first he thought that he would knock very loudly just to make *quite* sure . . . and while he waited for Piglet not to answer, he jumped up and down to keep warm, and a hum came suddenly into his head, which seemed to be a Good Hum, such as is Hummed Hopefully to Others.

The more it snows
    (Tiddely pom),

The more it goes
(Tiddely pom),
The more it goes
(Tiddely pom)
On snowing.
And nobody knows
(Tiddely pom),
How cold my toes
(Tiddely pom),
How cold my toes
(Tiddely pom),
Are growing.

'So what I'll do,' said Pooh, 'is I'll do this. I'll just go home first and see what the time is, and perhaps I'll put a muffler round my neck, and then I'll go and see Eeyore and sing it to him.'

He hurried back to his house; and his mind was so busy on the way with the hum that he was getting ready for Eeyore that, when he suddenly saw Piglet sitting in his best arm-chair, he could only stand there rubbing his head and wondering whose house he was in.

'Hallo, Piglet,' he said. 'I thought you were out.'

'No,' said Piglet, 'it's you who were out, Pooh.'

'So it was,' said Pooh. 'I knew one of us was.'

He looked up at his clock, which had stopped at five minutes to eleven some weeks ago.

'Nearly eleven o'clock,' said Pooh happily. 'You're just in time for a little smackerel of something,' and he put his head into the cupboard. 'And then we'll go out, Piglet, and sing my song to Eeyore.'

'Which song, Pooh?'

'The one we're going to sing to Eeyore,' explained Pooh.

The clock was still saying five minutes to eleven when Pooh

and Piglet set out on their way half an hour later. The wind had dropped, and the snow, tired of rushing round in circles trying to catch itself up, now fluttered gently down until it found a place on which to rest, and sometimes the place was Pooh's nose and sometimes it wasn't, and in a little while Piglet was wearing a white muffler round his neck and feeling more snowy behind the ears than he had ever felt before.

'Pooh,' he said at last, and a little timidly, because he didn't want Pooh to think he was Giving In, 'I was just wondering. How would it be if we went home now and *practised* your song, and then sang it to Eeyore to-morrow – or – or the next day, when we happen to see him?'

'That's a very good idea, Piglet,' said Pooh. 'We'll practise it now as we go along. But it's no good going home to practise it, because it's a special Outdoor Song which Has To Be Sung In The Snow.'

'Are you sure?' asked Piglet anxiously.

'Well, you'll see, Piglet, when you listen. Because this is how it begins. *The more it snows, tiddely pom—*'

'Tiddely what?' said Piglet.

'Pom,' said Pooh. 'I put that in to make it more hummy. *The more it goes, tiddely pom, the more—*'

'Didn't you say snows?'

'Yes, but that was *before*.'

'Before the tiddely pom?'

'It was a *different* tiddely pom,' said Pooh, feeling rather muddled now. 'I'll sing it to you properly and then you'll see.'

So he sang it again.

The more it
SNOWS-tiddely-pom,
The more it
GOES-tiddely-pom
The more it

GOES-tiddely-pom
On
Snowing.

And nobody
KNOWS-tiddely-pom,
How cold my
TOES-tiddely-pom
How cold my
TOES-tiddely-pom
Are
Growing.

He sang it like that, which is much the best way of singing it, and when he had finished, he waited for Piglet to say that, of all the Outdoor Hums for Snowy Weather he had ever heard, this was the best. And, after thinking the matter out carefully, Piglet said: 'Pooh,' he said solemnly, 'it isn't the *toes* so much as the *ears*.'

The Toys

CHRISTOPHER MILNE

Pooh, of course, was the teddy bear belonging to Milne's son, Christopher. Later Christopher Milne told the story (in The Enchanted Places*) of the soft toys which inspired his father to write of Pooh, Piglet and friends, and of how Ernest H. Shepard began his drawings.*

I must now introduce the toys.

Pooh was the oldest, only a year younger than I was, and my inseparable companion. As you find us in the poem 'Us Two', so we were in real life. Every child has his favourite toy, and every only-child has a special need for one. Pooh was mine, and probably, clasped in my arms, not really very different from the countless other bears clasped in the arms of countless other children. From time to time he went to the cleaners, and from time to time ears had to be sewn on again, lost eyes replaced and paws renewed.

Eeyore, too, was an early present. Perhaps in his younger days he had held his head higher, but by the time the stories came to be written his neck had gone like that and this had given him his gloomy disposition. Piglet was a present from a neighbour who lived over the way, a present for the small boy she so often used to meet out walking with his Nanny. They were the three round which the stories began, but more characters were needed and so two were invented: Owl and Rabbit. Owl was owlish from the start and always remained

Bears getting ready for the woods, or a Christmas party?

so. But Rabbit, I suspect, began by being just the owner of the hole in which Pooh got stuck and then, as the stories went on, became less rabbity and more Rabbity; for rabbits are not by nature good organizers. Both Kanga and Tigger were later arrivals, presents from my parents, carefully chosen, not just for the delight they might give to their new owner, but also for their literary possibilities.

So there they were, and to a certain extent their characters were theirs from birth. As my father said, making it all sound very simple, you only had to look at them to see at once that Eeyore was gloomy, Piglet squeaky, Tigger bouncy and so on. But of course there was much more to it than that. Take bears, for example.

A row of Teddy bears sitting in a toyshop, all one size, all one price. Yet how different each is from the next. Some look

gay, some look sad. Some look stand-offish, some look lovable. And one in particular, that one over there has a specially endearing expression. Yes, that is the one we would like, please.

The bear took his place in the nursery and gradually he began to come to life. It started in the nursery; it started with me. It could really start nowhere else, for the toys lived in the nursery and they were mine and I played with them. And as I played with them and talked to them and gave them voices to answer with, so they began to breathe. But alone I couldn't take them very far. I needed help. So my mother joined me and she and I and the toys played together, and gradually more life, more character flowed into them, until they reached a point at which my father could take over. Then, as the first stories were written, the cycle was repeated. The Pooh in my arms, the Pooh sitting opposite me at the breakfast table, was a Pooh who had climbed trees in search of honey, who had got stuck in a rabbit hole, who was 'a bear of no brain at all.'. . .

Then Shepard came along, looked at the toy Pooh, read the stories and started drawing; and Pooh who had been developing under my father's pen began to develop under Shepard's pen as well. You will notice if you compare the early Poohs in *Winnie the Pooh* with the later Poohs in *The House at Pooh Corner*. What is it that gives Pooh his particularly Poohish look? It is the position of his eye. The eye that starts as quite an elaborate affair level with the top of Pooh's nose, gradually moves downwards and ends up as a mere dot level with his mouth. And in this dot the whole of Pooh's character can be read.

That was how it happened. And when at last the final story had been written, my father, looking back over the seven years of Pooh's life, wrote his dedication. It was to my mother.

> You gave me Christopher Robin, and then
> You breathed new life in Pooh.

Whatever of each has left my pen
Goes homing back to you.
My book is ready, and comes to greet
The mother it longs to see–
It would be my present to you, my sweet,
If it weren't your gift to me.

A Christmas Fight off Seaford Head

REVD A.A. EVANS

Evans was vicar of East Dean, near Seaford, and writer of 'A Countryman's Diary' – a monthly article which he contributed to the Sussex County Magazine. *This piece comes from the first volume (1927) of the magazine.*

It was on Innocents' Day, December 28, in the year 1807, that the Downsmen who lived along the coast between Beachy Head and Newhaven saw a stirring sight, the fight of a small English coal-carrying vessel, a 'collier,' and a large French privateer, bristling with guns and other armaments.

England's great fleet, flushed with the glory of Trafalgar – it was two years after that great encounter – was elsewhere, following in the trail of a maritime combination Napoleon

Bonaparte had contrived, and for months the English coast, especially that of the Channel between Folkestone and the Needles, was being harried by well-armed, swift sailing French privateers, and almost every day there was a fight at sea with dour English trading vessels and light-of-heels Frenchmen.

On the morning of the 28th of December in that same year, the shepherds on the hills, and folk who in holiday mood sauntered about Seaford Bay, saw a stirring sight. A French privateer with white bellying sails hove in sight and began to cast her eyes about for British treasure. Just at that hour, when the mists of late morning were dispersing, a tramp vessel emerged from Newhaven steering a course for the port of London. Quickly the Frenchman was on her. Coals were of high value just then in France for Napoleon, in fierce jealousy, had shut up all his country's ports against British commerce and France nursed her patriotism with but scanty fuel.

The coal tramp was unarmed and made no resistance and in a very short time her men were battened down as prisoners of war and a prize crew put aboard to convey boat, men and 2,000 tons of choice Wallsend, to Cherbourg.

It all seemed so easy and the crowds ashore watched it with melancholy and terrified interest. Not a gun had cast shot.

Then to the excited spectators it seemed like an evil providence that just as the British boat had been sent off, flying the tricolour, another collier came in sight rounding Newhaven Head and right into the arms, as it seemed, of the French privateer. Quickly the French vessel moved to seize her prey and the call was trumpeted out to lower the Union Jack or fight for it. But now a gallant scene followed. The old black-looking collier, unlike the first vessel, carried a heavy gun or two with gunners who knew how to use them, and although the French vessel was lined with portholes which showed mouths of gleaming steel teeth, the only answer to the

Frenchman's summons was the bark of three guns with heavy shot and canister, which rent through the woodwork of the privateer and brought down some of its sail. At the same time every bit of bunting the collier carried was sent fluttering aloft. It was just a bit of cheek; it was a terrier for a moment getting its teeth into a mastiff just before being torn to pieces, or so it seemed. It only needed one broadside from the privateer to put the hulking collier out of action and send it to the bottom. But that broadside never came. Either the Frenchman hoped to secure a second prize as undamaged as the first, or, what was more likely, had been so confident of an unresisting capture that her guns were still limbered and before she had time to loosen and man them the collier had a second chance and used it. She was then close to the Frenchman and the guns this time played with deadly effect. For at this volley the shot was aimed below the privateer's water-line, tearing great holes, into which the water poured, and at the same time the sturdy collier bumped into her, cutting a deep vertical wound in her hull.

That was the end of the smart French clipper. In a few minutes she had sunk in the bay, carrying with her nearly 100 men, of which, – so swiftly did she submerge – the gallant little collier was only able with its dinghy to pick up five of the crew. The fight was witnessed by a huge crowd which had now gathered round the bay and on the hills from Newhaven to Seaford.

These were scenes and events fairly often repeated in those years of the long, desperate fight with France. Yet small, isolated instances like these hardly find their way into the literature of the war and are soon forgotten. This story is told from a short and terse account in the 'Lewes Advertiser' of that year.

Shepherd's Bush

TICKNER EDWARDES

Shepherds are so much a part of the Christmas story that it is rather sad to reflect that the Downland shepherds and the 'lookers' on the marshes are no longer familiar figures in our Sussex landscape. In this third extract from Tickner Edwardes, published in 1939 (four years after he retired as Vicar of Burpham), he records his visits to gorse patch and dewpond, features which, like the shepherds, have sadly all but vanished from the Downs.

December 27th

The great gorse patches on the Downs sing in the winter wind. In their shadows, the grass is still grey with rime, but on their sunny sides the sward is drenched with the melted frost, big trembling gouts of water pendent from every blade, and giving back the level morning beams in a thousand points of rainbow light.

A magpie starts out of the thicket, and then another – one seldom sees a single magpie at any time of year. The pair scurry off, filling the keen air with their sardonic cry. Then a green woodpecker breaks cover. Curiously faded looks his jerkin of Lincoln green as he loops by against the sodden, glowing hillside.

The rabbits that I saw from afar flicking their white topgallants round the copse, have gone to earth long ago. Only

the goldfinches remain. The little flock of a score or so keeps up its steady drifting from thorn to thorn, all the while giving out a low, sweet, desultory song.

December 29th

I was up at the dew-pond early – just as the sun was peering over the edge of the world and picking out every snow-clad hill-top around me with chevrons of rosy light.

But early as I was, the starlings were there before me. Creeping up the bank that surrounded the pond and stealthily looking over, I saw that the water was one solid sheet of ice, with half a dozen of the birds moping by its rim, evidently in dismay.

These flew away the moment my head appeared over the brow. But others came up on the wind, looked at the ice, gave it a hopeless, helpless peck or two, then made off. A minute or two later a green woodpecker came looping over from the thicket hard by. He, too, stared at the ice in bewilderment, going off at last.

Turning and gazing back as I trudged homeward, I saw a party of rooks streaming towards the pond, with the same disappointment in store.

The freezing of the dew-ponds is a serious matter for these downland birds, who depend on them for their water-supply.

December 30th

On the downs in the brilliant morning light the sheep were feeding among the gorse-brakes, and I would have stopped to look at them and listen a while to the drowsy music of the bells, only the fierce north wind would not let me halt for an instant: one had to keep steadily moving, or freeze to the marrow in its relentless icy flood. But the bark of a dog, and

then the sound of a human voice hailing me, turned my steps towards a neighbouring patch of furze. The old shepherd was sitting apparently right in the heart of one of the biggest bushes, as safely sheltered from the wind as he would have been in his kitchen at home.

It was a 'shepherd's-bush', in fact – such a haven as all South Down flock-tenders make for themselves here and there on their bleak, storm-swept rounds. The same spots are used year after year, and often generation after generation.

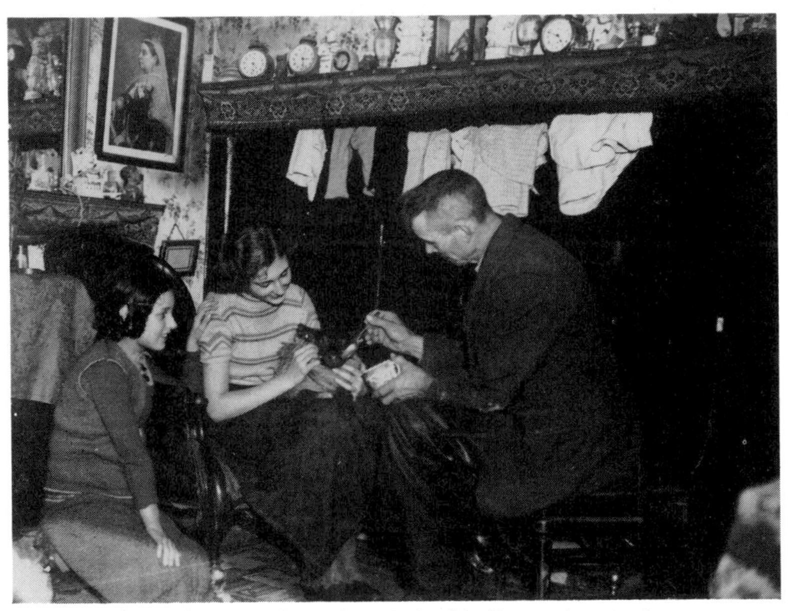

Doctoring a sick lamb at Eclesden Farm, Angmering, January 1938. Lambing was often earlier then with the first lambs being born at the beginning of the month – within the twelve days of Christmas

New Year at the Farm

JOHN HALSHAM

Christmas is a time for family reunion, yet for some a time when the loss or absence of loved ones is cruelly felt. In this sketch from Old Standards, *John Halsham discloses the pain of a Victorian Sussex farmer whose children have deserted the Weald for 'furrin parts'. 'Halsham' was the pseudonym of George Forrester Scott, whose books chronicled country life in mid-Sussex.* Idlehurst *(1898) was set in Lindfield, and* Lonewood Corner *(1907), Ardingly, the village where he died, aged eighty-four years, in 1937. After his death Arthur Beckett reported that Sussex had lost one of her finest writers.*

The lantern which had hung above the stall in the barn since twilight fell was taken from its nail at last; long shadows of the manger-bars, or a horned head and a man's stooping figure wavered up the walls and vanished in the hollow darkness of the roof; the heifer that had lain all day motionless and breathing hard among the straw was easier, and might safely be left for the night. The master and the cowman came out into the yard together, stretching cramped limbs and for the moment feeling their way like blind men, their eyes bleared with watching by the low light. The cowman, with half a mile of drenched field paths before him, took the lantern; the farmer crossed the yard and the little grass plot to the house door. With his hand on the latch he stopped to listen, as a swell of the wind brought the sound of bells up from the village beyond the hill. It was later than he had thought; they must be ringing the last peal for the old year – a thing he had never heard yet in all the time that he had been at Crosswaters Farm. Neither Peter Virgoe nor his wife was of the kind which sits up to watch the train of the departing year, and greet the new. The work of the farm was a linked and continuous whole which brooked no intervention on the part of the calendar: the day's labours had always won the night's rest; and the morning, whether it shifted the date of year or century, would come soon enough with the return of the inexorable duties. But tonight, so near as it was to twelve o'clock, he would for once keep the festival, and let in the new year. He would be in the fashion and meet it waking, like his neighbour Maclellan at High Beeches, and Saunders at the Lythe, and who were wont, with other northern invaders in that region, to make a night of it together, or like the people at the Manor House, where they always had the servants' ball. The wind that was sounding in the yew beside the porch suddenly lulled, and in the silence the music of the bells swelled from a confused murmur to a melodious clearness, every note of the coursing changes distinct, with the lingering chords and melancholy over-tones fleeting across the steady beat of the tenor. Peter Virgoe, who had been a ringer in his younger days, listened with head aslant to the well-handled peal, till he heard the seemingly interminable confusion of the changes roll out into the scale of 'rounds' again, and then pushed open the door and went into the living-room of the house. All was silent within; the air was full of a soft warmth, and the fine scent of the walnut-logs which, half burnt out, kept a red glow among the heap of feathery ashes on the hearth. There was light enough to show the shapes of things in the room to anyone

A Victorian card. Cards then often had images, such as a butterfly, which strike us now as unseasonal. Perhaps, given winter cold and the lack of central heating our Sussex ancestors liked to be reminded of warmer seasons

familiar with their places, to touch faintly out the lines of the wall-panelling and the sampler-frames and mourning-cards upon it, the long oak table and the dresser with its ware, the gun and the sheep-hook in a corner, the high settle beside the fire. Peter had left the door half open when he came in, and the night air, mixing its keen moist freshness with the warmth of the room, sent a little draught to the chimney and stirred a tongue of flame in the embers. The light shone on the old man's stooping figure as he stood with one foot on the hearthstone and his hand on the chimney-breast, showing such a form of lean ungainly strength as we figure Father Time under, an active hardness which seems to offer no holds to the assaults of age until, perhaps in the nineties, it gives way all at once. The blue neckerchief, the wide-skirted tail-coat and high leggings, with straws still about them from the vigil in the cow-stall, pictured the old-fashioned well-to-do working farmer, of a type that has almost vanished from the land. Peter's broad bald crown was encircled by a wreath of thick-curling grey hair; his face, ruddy and thin-featured, with a high-bridged nose and handsome mouth and chin, had an expression of alert wisdom, touched with a reflective air, a sense of spiritual refining: such mixture of elements is at times to be seen on the countenances of the older race, and on theirs alone.

As he leaned by the chimney the flame among the logs flickered and climbed till it threw a light that reached the tall clock in the farther corner, and showed that the old year had a quarter of an hour to run, a quarter or thereabouts, for they were always very easy about a few minutes this way or that at Crosswaters. As Peter waited by the hearth he took an ancient hour-glass from the mantel-board, turned it over and set it down on the table in the light of the fire, absently watching the thread of sand and the slipping, piling cone beneath it. There was nothing in the symbol which could trouble his thoughts, whether they looked backward or forward. Here, by the hearth which he had called his own for forty years, among the household goods which had come to be part of himself and not mere belongings, with the ordered fields lying about the house, the sheep and beasts in the fold and the yard under the quiet darkness, here he could find little room for over-anxious care. He was one of those people – happy, they would call themselves, if they ever gave a thought to the matter – who have filled up the tale of their days and have nothing left which can greatly concern them on this side of the grave. Thoughts which went beyond the bourne, serene rather than exalted, came often enough to Peter in those hours of busy-handed labour whose monotony makes such excellent retreats for the countryman's mind to muse in: to-night his meditations did not go beyond the bounds of time.

When it wanted a few minutes to the hour he crossed the room and set the door wide open. For a moment it was strange and a little discomforting to think of the house standing open to the world at such a time of night, long after it should have been safely barricaded with the ancient lock and the heavy oak spar. He called to mind, as he stood looking into the darkness, things that had crossed the doorstep, and things that were yet to come in or go out over it. No great shock of ill had entered during his time; no bad news of money or lawsuit lost, no breathless alarm of accident in the fields, no letter heavy with tidings of family disgrace. He remembered how his father, the day before he died, had walked in a little giddily, coming up at noon from the harvest-field and saying he would lie down for an hour till his head was better; the desolation of the loss had passed from Peter's mind; what remained was the memory of the strangely peaceful day of the funeral, the dazzling sunlight on the coffin as the white-frocked labourers carried it through the door and over the grass-plot before the house. The heavy oak rail which was used to strengthen the turn in the staircase against the weight of the bearers as they brought the body down was laid away on the top of the brew-house rafters, and waited till it should be wanted again for his wife's carrying-out, and his own. Their eight children had all gone out into the world happily enough, as most reckoned; married, gone to the Shires, to London, to Australia. Some of them they had never heard of for years; some came back to see them now and then, strangely changed in all their ways. The youngest daughter had paid a visit to the farm only so late as Christmas, bringing her husband, an engineer's foreman in Rotherhithe, and three of the grandchildren; and the party had been hard put to it to endure politely the third day at Crosswaters. They had gone; all the stir of the two generations of strangers in the house had passed by, and the place was as quiet as it was before the first child ever cried in it. She was strangely changed, was

A heart-shaped card depicting harebells, *c.* 1886

Milly; perhaps even Lucy in Queensland, if they were to see her again, might not seem so much altered. Lucy had always been the old-fashioned one; but she had not written for four years now; she would never cross the doorstep again; nor Harry, in the foundry at Leeds. And even if some chance were to bring them home again, it would hardly make any difference. Nothing to make any difference could ever come into the house now; the count of gain and loss was made up, even to the last outgoing.

From the firelit room the night had looked pitch-black through the open door; but as Peter stood on the threshold it showed light enough to disclose the familiar shapes of the farmstead and the fields. A fine rain was falling, but there was a bar of clear sky in the south, where a star or two shone with broad soft radiance. Peter had begun instinctively to think about the chances of ploughing the twelve-acre, with such weather holding, when the bells beyond the hill broke out with the clash which told that the new year was in. He went in and made the door fast behind him; he must get to bed and make the most of a short night. They would certainly be able to go on with the ploughing first thing in the morning.

A turn-of-the-century card: songster robins astride a bicycle. It is tempting to think that it may have accompanied the gift of a bicycle!

Christmas Song

BOB COPPER

This book ends as it began – with an old Sussex song collected and sung by the Coppers of Rottingdean. Bob Copper has a voice with a magic which speaks of all that Sussex, weald and down, once was.

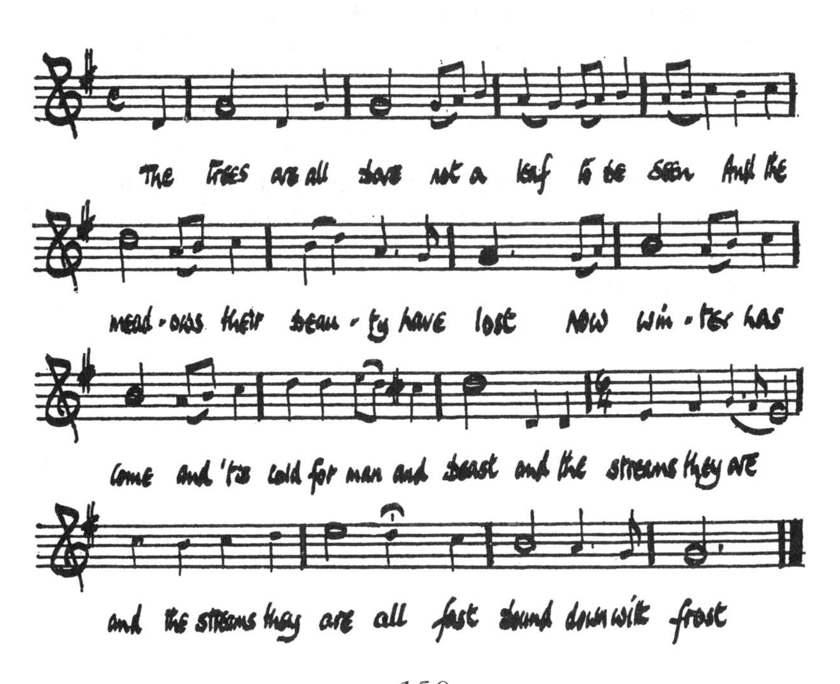

Christmas Song

The trees are all bare not a leaf to be seen
And the meadows their beauty have lost.
Now winter has come and 'tis cold for man and beast,
And the streams they are,
And the streams they are all fast bound down with frost.

'Twas down in the farmyard where the oxen feed on straw,
They send forth their breath like the steam.
Sweet Betsy the milkmaid now quickly she must go,
For flakes of ice she finds,
For flakes of ice she finds a-floating on her cream.

'Tis now all the small birds to the barn-floor fly for food
And gently they rest on the spray.
A-down the plantation the hares do search for food,
And lift their footsteps sure,
Lift their footsteps sure for fear they do betray.

Now Christmas is come and our song is almost done
For we soon shall have the turn of the year.
So fill up your glasses and let your health go round,
For I wish you all,
For I wish you all a joyful New Year.

Acknowledgements

My first and greatest debt of thanks is due to Bob Copper who has been an unfailing source of kindness, stimulation and wise advice. In particular I am most grateful to him for drawing my attention to the works of John Halsham and for his generous permission to use extracts from his own enthralling books, *A Song for Every Season* and *Early to Rise.*

My thanks are also due to the following for their kind permission to use material: extracts from *The Folklore of Sussex*, by permission of B.T. Batsford Ltd and Miss Jacqueline Simpson; Revd A.A. Evans' 'A Christmas Fight off Seaford Head' and Elizabeth Roberts' 'Bethlehem at Berwick' from the *Sussex County Magazine*, by permission of Beckett Newspapers Ltd (of Eastbourne); extract from Lilian Candlin's *Memories of Old Sussex*, by permission of Countryside Books; extract from Maude Robinson's *The Southdown Farm in the Sixties*, by permission of J.M. Dent and Sons Ltd; extract from E.F. Benson's *Mapp and Lucia*, by permission of William Heinemann Ltd; extract from *A Vicarage Family*, by permission of A.M. Heath and the Estate of Noel Streatfield; extract from Eleanor Farjeon's *Edward Thomas: The Last Four Years*, by permission of David Higham Associates Ltd and the Estate of Eleanor Farjeon; 'A Shepherd's Christmas' from Barclay Wills' *Bypaths in Downland*, extracts from Tickner Edwardes' *Neighbourhood* and *A Downland Year*, by permission of Methuen London; extract from Christopher Milne's *The Enchanted Places*, by permission of Christopher Milne and Methuen London; extract from A.A. Milne's *The House at Pooh Corner*, by permission of Methuen Children's Books and the Estate of A.A. Milne; Belloc's 'Courtesy', extract from his 'A Remaining Christmas', extract from his *The Four Men*, by permission of Peters, Fraser and Dunlop Group Ltd on behalf of the Estate of Hilaire Belloc; extract from R. Thurston-Hopkins' *Sussex Rendez-vous*, by permission of the Random Century Group and Skeffinton's; extracts from Sheila Kaye-Smith's *Sussex Gorse*, by permission of Mrs B Walthew and the Estate of Sheila Kaye-Smith; Andrew Young's 'Snow Harvest' and 'Christmas Day', by permission of his daughter Alison Lowbury; 'What is Winter?', by permission of Carcarnet Press Ltd and the Estate of Edmund Blunden. While every effort has been made to contact all copyright holders, in some cases this has proved impossible, for which I apologize.

Picture Credits

Mr Richard Pailthorpe, pp. 2, 22, 68; West Sussex Record Office, for the use of material from the George Garland Collection, pp. 6, 18, 27, 30, 41, 46, 49, 58, 59, 65, 78, 86, 89, 95, 100, 120, 125, 142; Worthing Museum, for permission to photograph cards and other items from the Museum collections, pp. 11, 15, 34, 36, 81, 99, 105, 117, 145, 148, 149; West Sussex County Library Service for permission to photograph Barclay Wills' sketch, p. 72; picture of *The Sussex Garland*, by kind permission of Mrs Pam Allsop, p. 112.